CW01302440

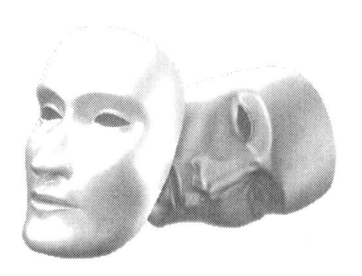

ACT
of
CONSCIOUSNESS

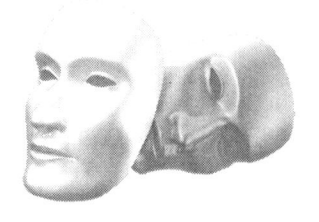

Adamus Saint-Germain

channeled by
Geoffrey and Linda Hoppe

Act of Consciousness

Copyright © 2015 by Geoffrey Hoppe

CRIMSON CIRCLE

Published by Crimson Circle Press,
a division of the Crimson Circle Energy Company, Inc.
PO Box 7394
Golden, Colorado USA
Contact: customerservice@crimsoncircle.com
Web: www.crimsoncircle.com

All rights reserved. Up to 250 words from this book may be quoted or reprinted without permission, with proper credit given to Act of Consciousness by Geoffrey Hoppe. Do not reproduce by any mechanical, photographic or electronic process.

Crimson Circle™, Adamus Saint-Germain™, DreamWalker™ and Shaumbra™ are trademarks of CCIP, Inc., Incline Village, Nevada USA. All rights reserved.

ISBN 1508902402

First Printing, March 2015

Printed in the United States of America

Cover Design: Geoffrey Hoppe
Book Design and Layout: Geoffrey Hoppe and Jean Tinder
Transcription: Gail Neube
Editing and Proofing: Jean Tinder and Maija Leisso

This book is dedicated to you. The fact that this book is in your hands means that something inside you has, or is, awakening. You're ready for the next step. It might not be what you thought it would be, but you're ready.

Now comes the time of discovery. Take a deep breath.

ACT of CONSCIOUSNESS
Contents

Author's Note 9
Adamus: The Act of St. Germain 11
Introduction 13

I. At the Threshold
  1. I Exist 17
  2. What is Enlightenment? 23
  3. Who is Responsible? 29
  4. In This Lifetime 33
  5. At the Threshold 35

II. Human and Divine
  6. Human Needs 41
  7. Four Primary Human Issues 45
  8. Comparing Human and Divine 49
    a. Passion vs. Needs
    b. Sensual vs. Emotional
    c. Experience vs. Action
    d. Radiance vs. Judgment
    e. Wisdom vs. Memory
  9. Reunion 63

III. Spiritual Physics
  10. How Energy Works 71
  11. Consciousness 79
  12. Consciousness and Thought 85
  13. It Comes to You 93
  14. Power is an Illusion 97
  15. Yo Soy el Punto 99

IV. It Is Time
    16. The Merlin Effect 107
    17. Walk Like A Master 111
    18. What Goes on Earth 115
    19. The Last Battle 119

Other Books 123
Other Courses with Adamus Saint-Germain 125
Additional Courses available through Crimson Circle 127
About Adamus Saint-Germain 129
About Geoffrey Hoppe 131
About Linda Benyo Hoppe 133
About the Crimson Circle 135
Glossary 137

Author's Note

Who would have thought? I used to ask myself that question every day. Who would have thought I would be communicating with angelic beings and Ascended Masters? As a young boy growing up in Wisconsin, I thought my life would follow in the footsteps of those I admired the most, especially my grandfather, a well-respected lawyer and judge.

My life took many twists and turns, filled with plenty of knots and tangles. I questioned many of my life choices, but mostly I questioned my fate. Why did certain things happen to me – whether I considered them to be good or bad – that seemed far beyond my control or choice? Why did life seem so fragile, yet why did the hand of destiny seem so firm and clear?

Along the way I was a writer, an advertising guy, a businessman, an inventor and an entrepreneur. I started and owned businesses, sometimes very successful and other times close to the flames of insolvency. I lived in Wisconsin, California, Texas and Colorado. As a marketing consultant, my greatest joy was helping clients effectively communicate their message. As an entrepreneur, my greatest achievement was co-founding an aviation telecommunications company that is now one of the world's biggest providers of Internet services on board business and commercial aircraft. I smile to think that I have two U.S. patents in "multi-dimensional communications." Who would have thought that I would be communicating on multiple dimensional levels, whether it was in the aviation business or with angels?

For the past 15 years, I've had the honor of being a messenger for a select group of angelic Masters: Tobias, Kuthumi lal Singh and St. Germain. Each of these Masters lived many lifetimes as regular humans before their enlightenment. They come back now to remind us of what we already know, but what we lost in the act of playing human. They remind us that there is nothing to achieve because it is already so. St. Germain uses the term "kasama." It means "the soul's desire." Kasama is the knowingness that you are already enlightened and ascended, beyond the boundaries of time, and now you are going through the experience of what it was like to realize it. It is already done, so now, how would you like to experience it?

Now, instead of asking myself "Who would have thought?" I just smile and realize that I already knew. I didn't know the details that would bring me to this place of communication with the Ascended Masters, and the details don't really matter. The fact is that my kasama – my soul's desire – already knew that I would be here at this place of being a multidimensional communicator. In spite of my upbringing and biological family, in spite of right or wrong decisions, even in spite of how I imagined my pre-awakened, non-enlightened self, it was my soul's desire to be here. There's nothing magical about it. Just allow.

Adamus: The Act of St. Germain

For the first 10 years of my channeling career, I worked with Tobias. I learned that he was my father in a long-ago lifetime, a story that is told in the biblical (apocryphal) *Book of Tobit*. Tobias was one of the best friends I've ever had, albeit an invisible one. He was loving and patient, and came to me nearly every day for channeling and personal spiritual guidance. When Tobias left in 2009, I started working with St. Germain of the Violet Flame. Well, kind of. It was a facet of St. Germain by the name of Adamus. Adamus Saint-Germain, as he prefers to be called and spelled, is an "act" of St. Germain. This facet of St. Germain brings new teachings and messages, through my wife Linda and I, to the Crimson Circle.

Adamus has no regard for alien space beings, conspiracy theories, gurus or other makyo (spiritual distractions). He is here to work with those who are choosing enlightenment while remaining in their physical bodies in this lifetime. He uses the name Adamus to differentiate his messages to the Crimson Circle from his messages through other channelers and materials. You could say that he "private labeled" himself just for the Crimson Circle work. By the way, the Crimson Circle is open, free and available to anyone who has checked their own "Ready for Embodied Enlightenment" box. There is nothing exclusive about it. Just make sure you're ready for some changes in your life before you check that box.

Adamus is an act or expression of St. Germain. He consciously chose this act because it's what is needed for those who place their enlightenment above all else. If that sounds selfish to you, Adamus will probably ask you to leave because there is nothing selfish about loving and honoring yourself. We've been taught to be in service to others (to place others first) at great expense to ourselves. The truth is that you can do more for others and the planet and the universe by loving yourself first. Then you become a Standard or example to others who are struggling for self worth.

Adamus can be provocative, aggravating, irreverent and occasionally rude. He doesn't care. If a glass of cold water over the head is what's needed to get someone out of their complacency, he'll gladly dump it on them. And he has. At the same time, Adamus is a brilliant professor. He's humorous, animated, engaging, wise and cleverly distracting.

And... it's all an act. He makes no apologies for acting because, as he points out, it's *all* an act. Humans act like they're human, with all their limitations and weaknesses, even though they're not. Spiritual seekers act like they are on the path to enlightenment even though they're not. They are already enlightened. People act like victims or villains, martyrs or teachers, children or adults, even men or women. But it's all an act. A child is already an adult in another point of Time, therefore they are not really only a child. They are just acting like a child until they transition into their act of an adult. You are no more an unrealized, trying-to-be-awakened spiritual seeker than you are an enlightened being. You are actually both, at the same time. You're already enlightened *and* you're also in the discovery of the journey of how you got there.

It's so simple that most people will shrug it off, lapsing back into their act of limitation. But a few will get it, embrace it, and act it. They will be enlightened, awakening and asleep at the same time, because they can be. One moment they'll choose to act small and the next moment they'll choose to act magnificent. Because they can. The next moment they will choose to simultaneously act limited and fully realized. Enlightenment isn't a destination. It is simply an act of consciousness.

Adamus continues to guide us every step of the way. He continues to entertain us and distract us so we don't get caught up in our own distractions. He lets you believe he's telling you something you don't already know, but he knows you know. It's all an act, an act of consciousness. Now the question is: where do *you* choose to put your consciousness?

Introduction

Life is an act. We act like humans and therefore we experience like humans with a litany of limitations, shortcomings and dramas that mask our underlying angelic consciousness. It is an unnatural act that we have come to accept as reality.

In *Act of Consciousness*, Ascended Master Adamus Saint-Germain begins by explaining the metaphysics of energy and defining the important difference between consciousness and energy. Adamus makes a clear point that we are beings of consciousness – not energy – and that the passion of our pure consciousness attracts energy from the unified field to manifest our reality. Adamus defines the four primary levels of energy including Core (soul), Crystalline, Cosmic and Earth, while educating the reader about how the various levels are used by our consciousness to manifest our stage-of-life.

Adamus implores the reader to *act* like a Master rather than acting like a less-than-perfect human. This act will literally change the type of energy that is attracted into the reader's life, and therefore change the reality theatre that he or she exists within. Some readers will question this approaching and say, "It's not real because it's just an act," to which Adamus would reply, "But everything in your life is just an act, so why not act like a prosperous, healthy and wise Master? This will change the theatre of your life, but the real question is, 'Are you really ready for a substantial change, or are you just trying to tidy up your current stage?'"

It is a remarkably simple and effective approach to an otherwise mental and laborious process of becoming your full potential. *Act of Consciousness* will amuse you and anger you, and it will certainly make you question your old beliefs about how reality is created and experienced. By the time you read Saint-Germain's last words, you will cry a few tears of joy and relief to know that life really is as easy as an Act of Consciousness.

Saint-Germain had many notable past lives, including that of William Shakespeare and Mark Twain (Samuel Clemens). These lifetimes gave him an appreciation for the theatre, acting and story-telling.

I

AT THE THRESHOLD

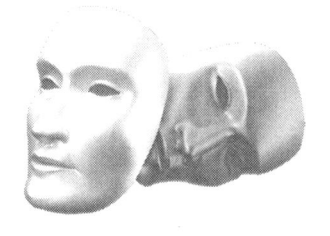

~ 1 ~

I Exist

I Am that I Am, Adamus, from the essence of Saint-Germain. Welcome to this living codex.

I exist. I exist!

These are the grandest words you can ever proclaim – "I exist!"

Oh, it is so simple. Would that every human had this realization deep within, in every moment and with every breath. But very few do. Very few feel or understand what this means – "I exist!"

Most humans simply live, realizing to a degree that they have consciousness, but rarely realizing that their consciousness lives, exists and experiences.

I exist; therefore, I Am. Ah! I exist; therefore, I can act. I can be anything I want. I can be Adamus. I can be Saint-Germain. I have been many different identities in many, many lifetimes because my consciousness, like yours, has the ability to act. Consciousness is not singular, nor is it fixed in a single expression.

Dear friend, take a good deep breath and feel into your own 'act of consciousness.' Your identity – this thing you try to fix and repair and adjust and amend – is just an act. It's not real. Or, more accurately, it's not the only reality. You've come to believe that it's real, that anything else you portray is either false or not quite honest. You dive deeper and deeper and deeper into what you assume is your identity, but it is just an act. It's a brilliant act, of course, but it's still only an act, an expression of something far grander.

Your mind will say, "I have to be real. I have to be truthful." But what you're doing right now isn't real. At least it's not the only reality or the only truth. You exist; therefore you can act, you can be and you can choose whatever you want to experience. You exist; therefore you can act. And when you act, energy responds to your consciousness.

The word "act" comes from the Latin word actus, meaning "doing," "action" and "thing done." It doesn't mean "faking it" or "pretending." The origin of the word "act" means "To Be."

Energy responds to the act of consciousness. This is a very literal statement. You act; energy responds. However, energy is very literal. If you act like a limited human, energy will respond in kind by delivering more limitation. If you act like your life has a lot of problems, energy will respond by giving you exactly that – more problems. It's all an act – a brilliant, beautiful act.

You see, all reality already exists. It's not like you're trying to create something out of nothing. Every reality and every possibility already exists, and you can choose which potentials to allow into your life. Which realities do you choose to act upon and experience? Everything is already there. You are whatever you're acting. Act like a student and you'll get lesson energy. Act like a Master and you'll get masterful energy.

In this book, we're going to explore and experience the Act of the Master. We'll take a look at the physics of energy, acting and mastery. It is my desire to show you how you can act and be anything you want – and I mean anything. I don't care about your family lineage, your education, your health, your level of abundance, your intellect, your I.Q. or anything else. None of that matters.

Please hear those words – *it doesn't matter*. Not your age, your looks, your weight or anything else because you can change it. You can act however you choose.

Ah! I feel such a longing from you – "Yes! Oh, please, Adamus! Please! I want this to be true!" And at the same time, "Ohhh, what if it's not? What if I can't do it? What if it's just more words?"

Dear friend, in the very hours you spend reading this living book you can have a life-changing experience. It's as easy as taking a deep breath and just being in it. I call it this "star hopping" or Yo Soy el

Punto (Spanish). "I am the point." Yo Soy el Punto. I Am the Point of Consciousness.

When I say that you have an opportunity for a life-changing experience, once again it brings up an interesting dichotomy. You think, "Oh yes! A life-changing experience! That's why I'm reading this book, to bring about changes in my life." But then the doubt comes in. "Oh, a life-changing experience? What's going to change? Will it be bad or good change? How about just a little change, nothing too drastic."

How about, my dear friend, a truly life-changing experience? It's not magic. You don't need to have special mystical abilities. It's just a matter of allowing.

Are you ready for your life to change, no matter what?

I am right here with you, every step of the way in this enlightenment. I'm here to help you to see a different perspective. Right now your perspective is very restricted. Your consciousness is very focused and limited. But, as you allow it to expand, you'll realize that enlightenment was always there; you just weren't tuned into it. You'll realize that all the energy was there. All the wisdom and the knowledge was there, just waiting for you. Everything was already there. All reality already exists; your experience depends on what you're dialed into, what act you are choosing.

Will it take a year or ten or fifty for you to start realizing your enlightenment? It's already there, now it's just a matter of realizing it. Your enlightenment is not a goal out there somewhere in the future. It's right here, simply waiting to be realized.

I can talk, push and provoke, but ultimately what it takes is someone finally allowing their enlightenment and then for others to see it. At that point I will work directly with those who have allowed their enlightenment, because there are going to be genuine challenges with staying in the physical body.

There's a strong seduction, particularly in the first year or two of enlightenment, to leave the physical body. You'll still have some aches and pains, feeling like you're carrying around a burdensome body, because you're also going to be aware of your new Light Body, and you'll wonder, "Why should I stay in this tired old physical body?"

The answer is: because the longer you stay in it, the physical flesh and bone won't feel so heavy anymore. And, as you stay on Earth as an embodied Master, others will see what is possible. When you become enlightened and immediately leave the planet, they don't have the ability to see you, touch you, or hear you; so I'll be working closely with those who choose to stay embodied on Earth as enlightened Masters.

* * *

You could have realized your enlightenment quite a while ago, lifetimes ago in fact. You could have just allowed, but you didn't. It's probably not that you were afraid of it, not that you weren't ready for it. No, the opportunity was there to realize your enlightenment a long time ago, but you didn't. Why?

You knew that going through enlightenment several lifetimes ago would result in physical death because the energies were very dense, very different. Back then it was much more difficult to stay in the body while going through the very intense process of embodied ascension. Part of you knew that you might only have a few brief moments to stay in the physical body, because with enlightenment comes a very seductive desire to leave the physical realms due to the harsh challenges of human existence.

You knew that you wanted to be an embodied Master, not a dead Master. You wanted to walk the Earth – feeling the ground beneath you, enjoying things like laughter, friendship, self-love, and experiencing life in joy – as a Master, so you said, "I'll wait," even though you could have done it back then.

You also said, "I want to experience my enlightenment with a group of kindred spirits. I want to experience it with others who are realizing their awakening on this planet at the same time. I don't need them for my enlightenment, but how much grander it will be to have others of common background and similar experiences to laugh the sacred laugh with, to eat the sacred food and drink the sacred wine together" – everything is sacred after you're enlightened! – so you said, "I'll wait." And here you are, in the lifetime of enlightenment.

It's actually the lifetime of realizing of your enlightenment, because it is already there. This lifetime is about the embodiment of your enlightenment.

I am here to remind you of this choice, of your soul passion for enlightenment; to remind you of its simplicity; to remind you that it's probably not what your mind has construed it to be for it is very, very different than what the human expects. I am here to remind you that right before enlightenment is the time of the greatest distractions – distractions that could easily, without exaggeration, take you four or five lifetimes to get through.

Therefore, I am here in joyful service to you – to prod and provoke, to amuse and entertain, and to remind you of your soul choice for the realization of your enlightenment.

~ 2 ~

What is Enlightenment?

What is enlightenment? Most people think enlightenment is when everything gets easy. It doesn't! Most people think enlightenment is when money suddenly flows in and everybody loves you and honors you and thinks you're sexy. Not necessarily. Problems don't necessarily go away, but there's a whole different perspective on problems and issues. Suddenly, they're not big monsters and demons anymore. Suddenly, they're just minor nuisances and irritations that you can easily walk away from.

Many people think that enlightenment is about becoming all-knowing, that an Ascended Master knows everything. No. In enlightenment, you actually know less than you ever did before, because the data and details become less important. Facts and figures are irrelevant. Math and science are nice but they are not really the basis of creation.

In enlightenment, there is simplification, reduction, distillation. You don't *need* to know everything. I am often asked about facts and figures of things that happened hundreds or thousands of years ago. I really don't know and I really don't care. I guess I could find out, but it's not so important.

Enlightenment is not about having psychic abilities such as seeing into the future. Yes, as an enlightened being, everyone will flock to you and want to know what's going to happen tomorrow. And I can already tell you the answer to give them: tomorrow will be much like today because humans tend to follow patterns. They get into ruts and really don't make very many life-changing choices. They like to make little adjustments – a little more money, a little more bread and circus – but they shy away from real changes.

Rather than suddenly knowing or having everything, enlightenment is *integration*. You integrate all of your aspects, as well as your soul being and human being, into the I Am. The integration comes when you have compassionate acceptance of yourself. Integration occurs when you love yourself, without exception or reservation. With this love and acceptance, all the parts, pieces, aspects and ghosts of yourself find their way back home for integration. You feel fulfilled rather than fragmented. Instead of feeling like pieces of a puzzle, you feel whole.

Enlightenment is freedom. There are many things that keep you from freedom, things like allowing yourself to get stuck in very old energies and traumas, or allowing other people to dictate your life. And you're still in the mind, one of the greatest illusions and limitations. All of these things cause a lack of freedom.

In the integration and freedom of enlightenment, suddenly you find that nothing really matters.

Now you ask, "But if nothing matters then what's the purpose?" There actually is no purpose. There is no meaning of life.

Oh, that takes a little air out of the sails! But you see, there *is* no meaning of life, and an enlightened being realizes it's simply about experience. It doesn't need any big meaning. Life is just for the joyful experience, the act of living consciousness.

You don't *need* a purpose! You can be here in abundant awareness to simply enjoy the act of living.

The human mind has been conditioned to believe that it has to have purpose. You must have a reason for getting out of bed in the morning. You must have a reason for your life. You must have goals. In enlightenment, there are no goals! Ah, think of the freedom in that. When there's no purpose, then there's no reason to try to find the meaning of life. In fact, the more you try to find it, the less you will actually discover. Life was not intended to have meaning. It was intended to be a playground of experience. If there is any meaning whatsoever, it would just be an ever greater experience of loving yourself. That's it.

Enlightenment is the freedom from goals, from purpose, from meaning, and it's *never* boring.

When I say these things about enlightenment, so often there is a reaction – "Oh, it sounds so boring!" It is not at all, because suddenly you're living a very multidimensional, colorful, high definition life of experience, rather than a flat, linear, 3D life of drudgery. Suddenly, you're aware of so much more – other realms, other dimensions, and the ability to act and play and experience without getting wounded, fragmented, tortured or forgetful of who you really are.

* * *

Enlightenment. You've been studying it, working on it and suffering through it for many, many lifetimes. If you are reading this book, perhaps you are one who has chosen *this* lifetime to finally realize and experience it. It's wonderfully thrilling, but it's also extremely frightening. You have probably already encountered some of the demons and dragons of enlightenment that bring up your deepest, darkest issues and deep fears – beyond most fears you've ever felt.

Why? Because everything that is stuck and unresolved within has to come back into balance, so it comes forward. That's why you have flashbacks of suppressed childhood memories or encounter "ghosts" of yourself from the past. Then you try to heal them and process them and do all sorts of things to get rid of them, but they are there for a reason. The ghosts from your past are coming back, not to be fixed or repaired, but to be integrated. They're coming back because part of you knows you're at the threshold of enlightenment and it's time to integrate. Nothing is left behind, no parts or pieces. Every single particle of you comes back for integration.

You come now, after many, many lifetimes, to this point of enlightenment and oh, it is a vicious warrior. There is nothing airy-fairy about enlightenment. It has nothing to do with "New Age." It is a vicious, ruthless warrior. It is also a beautiful, sensual beautiful lover. It is your worst enemy; it is your best friend.

This time in your life right now is the best, most beautiful of times. I know it's also one of the most difficult times you've ever had, but I want you to remember that it is truly the best of times.

I know there are days when you feel like you're being put through a grinder, days when you feel pulverized by yourself, when you feel like you're being ripped apart limb by limb and thought by thought. But it is truly the best of times as well, because it's the time that you've chosen for integration, freedom and enlightenment.

Many spiritual seekers ask me, "Am I going to do it in this lifetime? Am I going to realize my enlightenment?" It's totally doable – and it's totally up to you. Some ask if they have the wherewithal to endure it, because they feel at the very end of their energy. They don't even know if they have the stamina to get through the next day let alone the grueling step into enlightenment. The answer is... absolutely, you do.

During our time together in the pages of this book, you'll realize that it actually doesn't take any work. It doesn't require any stamina. You've resisted so many things in life and this has exhausted you. Now, as you release the resistance, the energies naturally rebalance and then it doesn't take the last of your energy. It doesn't call for your strong will and determination to realize this thing called enlightenment.

Enlightenment is the natural evolution for every souled being.

You cannot study your way into enlightenment. There's not any book that can give you the code or the key to enlightenment. You've studied many things in the past – philosophy, religion, the mysteries – and they served you at the time. But none of them have the answer for you now. Not the Bible, the Koran, the Torah, or any other holy book, because they were all written by unenlightened beings. Smart beings, nice beings, but not enlightened beings.

You will discover that enlightenment comes naturally. It takes no effort. You don't have to use your willpower or determination. There's nothing to force. So often I see you working at your enlightenment, pushing at it, efforting with it. No, dear friend. It doesn't take any effort, and all the struggle will actually become a distraction.

Enlightenment comes with *allowing*. Allowing is like surrender, and that's a hard thing to do. It's a total surrender to your Self – not to some unknown God, but to your Self. In surrendering there is an innate fear that something might go wrong, that you'll be hurt. Your mind and your aspects are happy to remind you of all the mistakes and bad decisions you've ever made. They'll say that if you surrender and allow, your defenses will be down and dark energies and entities can come in. So you resist.

You think about letting go, but you don't actually allow it. You think about surrendering, but then do it in very small increments. You continue holding onto the illusion of your identity. Through the ages I've had so many students who think that enlightenment or spirituality is about understanding their identity. It is not at all, other than to understand that the identity is just an act.

Along the journey to enlightenment, you'll go through the phase of diving deep within yourself, going into the inner discovery. But, at a certain point you'll realize you're just diving deeper into an identity that's really just an act. You've been trying to solidify and validate your identity, to make it even more real and correct, but, at some point, you'll realize it's time to surrender to your Self. It's time to take a deep breath and simply allow.

It sounds easy, but it's the most frightening thing a human will ever do. It sounds so simple, but yet you'll find a million reasons not to do it.

You are finally here at the threshold of enlightenment because of your determination, your strong will, and your damn stubbornness. That's a good thing up to a point. You've endured. Oh my god, how you've endured one thing after another – assault, battery, torture, beating yourself up, letting others beat you up, everything else – looking for the answers. You've endured, and I give you an honorary medal for endurance. But now it's time to crush that medal, because willpower and endurance is not going to bring enlightenment. It brought you to this point, but now it's time to realize that you don't have to force or push or work at anything. Nothing. At the threshold of enlightenment, it's all about *allowing*.

~ 3 ~

Who Is Responsible?

Here's a big question for you:
Who is responsible for your enlightenment?
Think about it for a moment before you read on.

What answer did you find?
My answer, which doesn't have to be yours, is: your soul.

Your soul, your divinity, whatever you want to call it, is responsible for your enlightenment. Just feel into that for a moment. What a tremendous release! You, the human aspect, don't have to figure it out. You *can't* figure it out, and that's the little hidden secret to this.

The human aspect has no concept whatsoever of true enlightenment or ascension. It simply cannot conceive of it, other than to imagine a greater, grander version of itself. The human aspect, with its mental focus and survival instinct, has certain structures, needs and desires, and they have nothing to do with going beyond. Your human aspect is not seeking enlightenment or even more awareness. In fact, the human identity will actually work against you at times because it does not understand awareness or enlightenment. It understands mental activities, survival, emotions; but it does not understand enlightenment. It couldn't possibly understand because it was never intended for this purpose, and it certainly should not be burdened with trying to figure it out.

One of the pitfalls of many of the humans who are coming close to enlightenment is the belief that they, the human, must *achieve* it. They get involved in programs and goals related to their enlightenment, trying to manage all the minutia and the details when they don't even understand enlightenment, how the energies are working or what's really happening in their life.

The human aspect gets very involved in enlightenment because it feels the passion for that coming from the soul. The human aspect also is a little tired of the tedium of everyday life and wants something different, such as a better life, so it adopts this thing called enlightenment, thinking of it as a means to a better life. Enlightenment is *not* a better life. It is a totally *new* life, completely different than anything the human has ever experienced.

The responsibility for your enlightenment lies with your soul, your divinity. You, the human aspect, still not fully aware of how all this is working, are being asked to just go with the experience in total trust and allowing; to understand and assume that everything that's happening is part of your enlightenment. Allow your soul to do the work.

When you have bad, challenging, difficult and low energy days, don't get caught in the mind and think, "What am I doing wrong? What new class should I take? What new makyo (spiritual distraction) can I drench myself in?" Instead, trust that the enlightenment is the passion of your soul and therefore can never be lost or defeated. You're just going through part of the experience.

The wisdom of your I Am totally understands what is unfolding. It is beyond time and already knows it has realized its enlightenment while embodied here on Earth. And now your soul, through you its human aspect, is just going through the experience of what it was like.

Take a deep breath, dear friend, because this is a tremendous release! Let go of the pressure to find enlightenment. Let go of trying to figure it out. Let go of the burdens that you've placed on yourself, the guilt and the doubt about getting it wrong. Your soul is the one becoming enlightened in this physical reality; you're just along for the ride.

This is such a beautiful, simple concept. As I have said many, many times, enlightenment is a totally natural occurrence. You can't study for it or force it to happen; it just happens. You can study spirituality and philosophy up to a point, but then let it all go. True enlightenment is a natural process that you must simply experience.

In fact, it is so natural that when your human self tries to control or direct it, getting in the way of a very natural phenomenon, it's going to hurt. You're going to feel like things are being ripped and torn from you, like you're hanging on for dear life. It will feel like you're being sucked into an abyss, rather than gracefully flowing into your enlightenment. So please let go of trying to manage your enlightenment.

It is the soul – the divine You – that is responsible for your realization, and it doesn't need to plan or manage or figure anything out. It simply *realizes* the enlightenment. It's very simple. You can relax.

Relax into your enlightenment.

~ 4 ~

In This Lifetime

As an awakened human, you've probably had between 850 and 1,400 lifetimes in a physical body on this planet, and have most likely been here since the early times of Mu (Lemuria) or Alt (Atlantis). You came to this planet as a representative of your spiritual family, and now here you are, after a thousand or more lifetimes, in the grandest time ever seen on this planet – this time of awakening.

If this book is in your hands, you are now choosing to realize your "I Am" consciousness, probably well in advance of most other humans. It doesn't make you better – maybe a little crazier or more adventuresome – but you're choosing to do it ahead of most other humans. Their opportunity will come, but it will be different than your enlightenment because very few have done it before you.

In the many millions of years of history of this planet, only about 9,000 beings have ascended, have realized their I Am Presence. That's not very many at all, but now a global awakening is underway. Millions of humans from every part of the world are beginning to awaken to their spiritual origins, often doing it very quietly, unassociated with any specific group. It may take them several more lifetimes to actually realize their enlightenment, but there will also be many – perhaps even you – who will realize enlightenment in this lifetime *and* stay in the physical body.

Ascension is a very personal process. Nobody will ever be able to write the definitive guidebook for awakening or a "How To" book for becoming enlightened. They may share their own story, but there can never be a single book that shows how awakening or enlightenment is done because it is an intensely personal, very deep and very transformational process.

You are part of the first wave of this group of humans who are awakening in this New Energy era. The ones who come after you aren't going to go through the levels of doubt, consternation, chaos and drama that you've had to deal with, because you'll have already plowed through mass consciousness, pushed beyond old paradigms, and pressed through that invisible yet very seductive barrier that would keep one in the 3D world. The work you're doing is blazing the trail for the many who will come after you.

You hear the words, but I don't think you even realize what you're doing for yourself and, ultimately, for this planet and all of creation. I know that you doubt yourself. You often think of yourself as small, puny, weak or ineffective. But one day, you'll get the perspective that I have and you'll see what you're really doing.

Sometimes, in our Ascended Masters Club of some 9,000-plus ascended beings, we call it "Against All Odds." Somehow, against all odds, you're actually doing it and it's amazing.

It's not happening through your determination or will power, because you would have been crushed a long time ago by the rigors of awakening. It's not your mental competence that's keeping you on the path of enlightenment, so what is it?

What keeps you going when others have dropped out? What is it that makes you pick yourself up and keep going when you don't think you have any more energy, hope or desire to go on? Even in the darkest moments, something still rises up from within you and carries on.

Sometimes you attribute it to angels, spirit guides, or even once in a while to me. But it's actually You. It is something that rises up within you, your soul's passion for its realization of enlightenment. And now here you are, in your awakening, in the most promising time in the history of humanity.

~ 5 ~

At the Threshold

I was just like you. I was aware of standing at the threshold of enlightenment. It wasn't fear that kept me from stepping across. I had already said goodbye to my human lifetimes. I had said goodbye to the limitations of mental expression. I had said goodbye to my family, to most of my dear friends, even to my dogs.

I was right on the threshold of enlightenment and kept saying, "Any day now, any day." But I waited. I waited intentionally, because I so loved the human experience! As I waited, I let myself remember all of the things I had done, the people I had met and the places I had visited. But I was remembering them in a different way.

You see, the past is not what you think it was, and events did not unfold the way your mind remembers them. As you approach the threshold of enlightenment, you start feeling back into your lifetime – not thinking, but feeling – and you realize, just like I did, that the events of your life were much different than what your mind remembered. You realize that while your memory held on to the traumas and difficulties, there was actually an incredible beauty and light in *everything* you experienced.

So, I waited at the edge of enlightenment. It was exciting. It felt similar to being right on the edge of a sexual orgasm and holding it. Oh! You just don't want to go over the top. It's such a beautiful tension in that moment, why go all the way just yet? You let that tension, that excitement, that sensual experience build and build until you just can't hold it anymore. And then, ahhhhh! The symphony of life. The grand orgasm.

So, I waited. I held off for many years so I could feel back into my life, so I could feel the warmth of all of my experiences without regret, without saying, "Oh, I wish I had done it different." Your life experiences generally unfold within a limited reality and it's only later that you can really feel and re-experience them with a whole new perspective.

I waited and waited. I left society and went off to live by myself in the forests of northern Germany. I wanted to say goodbye to nature, dear Lady Gaia. Oh, she had been such a good friend (and sometimes an unlikely enemy) along the way in my many, many lifetimes on this planet. Being in nature reminded me of the beauty of seeing how life comes alive in this reality. It reminded me of the way this planet was infused with life energies long before angels or humans ever got here, how it birthed the forests, the trees, the waters, the air, the plant and animal life *for you*, for your experience here.

I connected deep into the Earth, knowing that it was a symbol for my physical lifetimes, because I wanted to take the essence of my physical body with me into ascension. When one ascends they can integrate the essence of their physical body with them so they can re-imagine it at any time, even to the degree of being able to re-manifest it on Earth from time to time.

I spent a long time reconnecting and integrating all aspects of myself. It balanced my energies and it reconnected me with the beauty of bringing life to life. After enlightenment a Master does that in many other realities, in many other parts of the cosmos. They bring life to life.

When I could not hold back any longer, when it was the day, my day, I took my body with me. It basically evaporated; nothing left behind but a very nice suit of clothes that fell to the ground. No bones, no flesh, no blood. It was all integrated.

Now, some would say that a strange phenomenon happened when my body disappeared. Some would say that it's buried somewhere. But the fact is that your body doesn't have to just decompose in the ground. It can literally integrate with you when you go into your ascension.

You take it with you for a lot of reasons, but primarily because it was *you* in your final precious lifetime on Earth. And, when you leave nothing behind, you take all the attributes of physical reality with you in your continuing journeys. Having the physical body integrated with you allows you to recreate it any time you wish in your journeys beyond the physical realms.

Yes, I waited. And perhaps you are also waiting – just waiting for the day, *your* day. Maybe you are waiting out of fear of what may happen next or simply because you want someone else to go first, to see how they did it. You might be waiting because you are enjoying the beauty of life, and why not? You're waiting for the day, but in the meantime allowing yourself to have fond memories and feelings for your many, many lifetimes on Earth.

It is kind of bittersweet, this waiting. Oh, some of the lifetimes, even this one, were very, very difficult, brutally tough – like a ferocious warrior or an angry dragon crushing you – but other times so exquisitely beautiful. It can be overwhelming to feel it all drawing to a close.

I'm not trying to push you into enlightenment, but I want you to realize that it's not at some remote distance. It's not in some far-off day. It can be right here, right now in this moment. Or, you can remain in the experience, on the edge of this great orgasmic experience of enlightenment for a while. That's fine too, but realize that you're doing it by choice.

You came into this life for your enlightenment. You still wonder about it – if you're ready, if you've done enough or learned enough or released enough – but yes, absolutely. You are ready.

II

HUMAN AND DIVINE

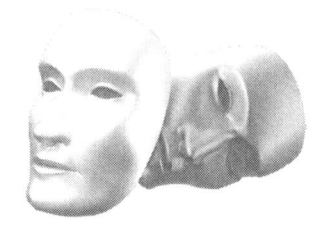

40

~ 6 ~

Human Needs

Before we get into more information about enlightenment, I'd like you to take a few moments to breathe and to feel.

Take a moment now to connect with your human self, your human needs, your human desires.

Now be aware of your soul, the part of you that has seemed so distant for so long. It is coming closer now, responding to your choice for integration.

Take a deep breath.

The soul is listening right now. You've awakened it, brought it in a little closer. It is listening.

This is a time to be very clear with your soul about your human needs. I'm talking about the elemental basic needs like health, abundance, a relationship with the soul, love of self.

Make it very clear what your human needs are, even if you think they are mundane things like a different job or more time by yourself. The soul *will* respond. It doesn't always really understand the human's needs because it only sent an aspect of itself to Earth to live in human form with human logic and limitations. It doesn't get involved in the details because it's just distilling the wisdom from your life. Every experience you have is accepted by the soul without judgment, distilled into wisdom and brought back into itself. The soul just doesn't get caught up in the human details.

But now the human details become important because the soul and the human are actually integrating back together, right here in the physical body on Earth. And if the soul is going to be here with you, it's important for it to understand you, the human, and to know what your needs are. For instance, the need for abundance. Ah, be grandiose with it! Health, self-worth, all of these things – be bold and let the soul know what you need and desire.

Don't just ask for it or wish for it. Demand it. Take a deep breath and say, "Soul, this is what we need. Bring it on!" and then feel into the deep passion of the soul. It is the passion to be, to experience, to live, and it's that *passion* that brings forth the abundance, the health, and anything else you need.

Take a good deep breath.

Part of the purpose of this exercise is making it clear to *yourself* what you need, what you really want and choose. Oftentimes, there is kind of a fogginess about that. You know what you *don't* want, but you're not always sure what you *do* want.

In the true act of consciousness, you just ask for it, demand it, allow it and receive it.

Take another deep breath, and again.

The soul can feel that the mind has quieted down now, at least for a few moments. It says, "Okay, I'm ready to listen. Tell me a little bit more about what you're going through. Tell me a little more about what you need. With passion, together we'll make it happen."

Take a few more deep and conscious breaths.

Now take this moment to feel your soul. Not to honor or worship it, but to intimately be with it, to feel it. You've been talking to it saying, "Hey, soul, there are some of my needs." Now make it very clear.

When somebody crosses over to the other side and has an encounter with their Soul Self, they'll often be in tears saying, "Oh! It was such a tough life. I couldn't pay my bills. My house was repossessed and I nearly starved. It was terrible!" The soul meets them with an astonished look and says, "Why didn't you tell me?!" And then the human has the astonished look and says, "I thought you knew!" The soul says, "Never assume that I know everything."

So, pause your reading and make it clear right now.

Take a good deep breath.

* * *

There isn't really a big long list of things that you need. It's pretty basic. The soul doesn't always understand the needs of the human, so make your needs clear to the I Am.

The soul is like the sun, up there just shining away, rather oblivious to what's happening down here on Earth. It really doesn't have any agenda other than to shine. It loves shining. It shines all day and all night. It shines all the time, whether you can see it or not, and doesn't care if the trees and the grass accept its light. It doesn't care whether you get sunburned or protect yourself from its rays. The sun doesn't care if it's too hot or if something is blocking its warmth. It's just there in its radiance and expression. Its passion is to shine.

That's how your soul is – it's just there. It's the I Am, the core consciousness, always there. It doesn't differentiate between a good day or a bad day. It doesn't even know it's a day. It just is. Always shining.

The human has needs based on survival, based on desires for comfort, pleasure and no pain. Therefore, it is the human that needs to be very clear – you with your Self – about your needs.

There are no outside beings on any level that bestow gifts to the human. None whatsoever. There is not an Akashic Record that keeps track of whether you've been naughty or nice. It is entirely up to you to be clear with your Self about your needs.

Perhaps you have felt guilty about having your own needs and desires because you're used to taking care of everybody else. Perhaps you've been told that there's only so much of anything to go around and that if you take care of yourself first it means you're selfish. It is interesting programming, an impressive game, but it's just not real – unless you want it to be.

Actually defining your human needs can be an interesting exercise because there tends to be a lack of clarity about what you really want. When I refer to human needs, I'm not talking about lofty metaphysical, ethereal concepts. I'm talking about money in your pocket, a car to drive, a beautiful home, not worrying about your bills, all these things. Don't feel guilty about them. Feel blessed that you have them. If nothing else, feel how it's just a game of "How abundant can I be? How healthy can I be?" Play with it. There is no need for you to carry the burden of poverty and lack on your shoulders, just like there's no need for you to take on the responsibility for your enlightenment.

Remember, the human self really doesn't know anything about enlightenment and couldn't figure it out if it tried. It can't plan, design or implement enlightenment, so please, leave that to your divinity, but do allow it into your life. Understand that as you allow the enlightenment, things are going to swirl and change and rebalance and reorder. Instead of saying, "Oh, damn, what's happening? Oh, poor me!" say, "Wow, I'm blessed! Life is changing!" Sometimes there will be bumps in the road, sometimes even big obstacles, but they will pass.

~ 7 ~

Four Primary Human Issues

Human issues – and therefore human needs – can be put into four main categories: Abundance, Health, Relationships and Self-worth.

Abundance

You deserve abundance. Period. So many humans, especially those on a spiritual path, have a history of holding back on the abundance, of not allowing it into their lives. There are many reasons for this, but they don't matter anymore. There is plenty of abundance available, now is the time to receive it. I'll talk about how to attract it, then it's up to you to actually receive it.

I don't care what type of background you come from, if you've been bankrupt two or three times, or whatever the story; there is abundance for you. Don't let anything get in the way of that. Abundance is available and waiting for you.

You *need* abundance. As an embodied Master you need money, material resources, a good home and a reliable automobile, so please allow yourself to receive it.

Don't worry about taking too much abundance, because there is more than enough to go around. Everyone can even have more than enough, if they choose, but the right amount of abundance will be there at the absolute right time.

Health

Health is the experience of balance in physical embodiment. You want and need a healthy body. There's no need to have a lot of aches and pains. They will accumulate from time to time, just from being in this dense reality (which is why I recommend taking three days to yourself each month, to rejuvenate your body), but they don't need to be an issue.

Deep breathing is one of the best things you can do for your biology. Being in water, whether it's taking a bath or swimming in the ocean, helps to release the toxins that build up in the body. It doesn't matter if you have cancer, diabetes, heart disease or anything else, these things can be released. They truly do not serve you anymore.

Your body has the ability to rejuvenate itself, to bring in youth and vitality. Right now, the body and mind are very inefficient in how they use energy. As you open up to more energy, you'll find that it takes very, very little to fulfill the needs of the body.

It's easy to get caught up in diets and rules about what you should and shouldn't eat, what's good or bad for you. But remember that these rules are coming from people who are not in the same state of consciousness as you. Their thoughts about food might be fine for them and even for many other people, but listen to *your* body. It will tell you what it needs. It may not make sense at first, but your body will tell you when to eat, what to eat and what not to eat, and it will change on a regular basis. Please don't get caught up in dieting, because it's going out of trust with your body and it will respond accordingly. The body's anayatron (the biological communication network) will stop its natural communications while you play the diet game.

Relationships

While the soul doesn't necessarily need a relationship, the human still tends to have that need or desire. The first and best relationship is with yourself, but there's also a strong desire to have relationship with others, to share and experience with other humans.

For those coming into their spiritual awakening, relationships are one of the toughest issues. You're moving out of karmic relationships – in other words, relationships with friends, family members and loved ones that were based on previous lifetimes – and going into a whole different type of relationship. The new relationships will be much more free, have little or no energy feeding, and you'll actually need far fewer of them.

You'll still be able to interact with other humans, but I dare say that, at times, you're going to find them tedious and aggravating. You're going to find it more and more difficult to be in crowds or with a lot of other people. There's such an energetic noise and you'll be more sensitive than ever to other people's energies, so listen to your own desire for solitude.

That being said, there's still the human desire for intimate relationships, so choose a relationship that is healthy for you and mutually beneficial. Be in a relationship that will inspire you and allow you to inspire others. Gone are the days of the old entangled karmic relationships. They were somewhat interesting, they had a lot of drama, but you don't need them anymore.

Self-worth

Compassion for self is a human need. It's a soul need as well, but definitely a human need, for how can you do all these other things – have the abundance, the health, the relationships – without honoring and respecting yourself?

That means to forgive yourself, to have compassion for yourself, to accept all that has come before, no matter what. That's a tough one for many humans, because they still want to hold those images and memories of the past. They keep them like pictures on the wall, reminders of what not to do or of what they have done wrong. But please take all those pictures off you inner wall now, because they are only illusions. They are not full or even accurate portrayals of what really happened.

As you take each picture off the wall, as you forgive yourself and let these things go in total compassion, a new picture will appear, as if by magic. It will be holographic, not limited to what the mind has remembered, and it will provide a fuller, clearer and more compassionate account of the past experience.

If there's anything to remember, if you have anything adorning the walls of your spiritual house, it should be just a plaque to yourself, a reminder that you've come too far to ever do those types of things again. You'll never again act in low consciousness. You'll never again act without compassion. You've gained too much wisdom and your consciousness is far too expanded to ever go back to crimes or hurting others. You're just not going to do that, so you can take all those guilt-ridden pictures off the wall and simply put a reminder to yourself that it's never going to happen again.

It's important to be clear with yourself about what you need going into enlightenment. You don't want to go into it half abundant, half healthy or in a half-hearted relationship. Be clear with yourself and command it to be so. You don't have to define the amount of money; just allow full-on abundance, full-on health, beneficial relationships.

Remind yourself often of this, because you're going to slip and go back into old patterns. Remind yourself clearly that this is what you're choosing and that you're ready for it, and the energies then will come in to serve you.

When you're not clear, when you don't know, when you're just waiting for something to happen, the energies will respond accordingly. Not much will happen. If you're very clear, committed and real about it, these things will come your way, no matter what.

~ 8 ~

Comparing Divine and Human

You are a soul being in the midst of a human experience. I think you realize that. There's ultimately no difference between the human mental being and the I Am or the soul, but you are living in the illusion of separation. You're living within the different parameters of each part, which is very, very difficult. It is sometimes the reason you experience physical pain, because you're evolving into your light body while remaining in biology. It's the reason you go through a lot of mental challenges and doubts, because you're getting out of the mind while still trying to use it.

So now let's talk about the five primary differences between your human self and your divine self. When I say, "Leave it to your divinity," it's important to know what I'm talking about.
 a. Passion vs. Needs
 b. Sensual vs. Emotional
 c. Experience vs. Action
 d. Radiance vs. Judgment
 e. Wisdom vs. Memory

Divine has Passion

The soul has tremendous passion to know itself, to experience itself and to be itself. This passion isn't for anything outside of itself. It is for itself alone. You could say it started with the passionate question, "Who am I?" and, ever since, that passion has led the soul on this amazing journey. It is not a passion to understand the cosmos or other souled beings; the passion is for your Self.

I ask you now to take a moment and feel into that passion. It is the inner flame, the desire of the soul. It's always been there. And when the human self goes into despair and darkness, not knowing how it's going to survive another day, it is this original passion that comes forth and inspires the human to keep going.

The passion of your divinity is the cause of creation.

The intense passion of the soul ignites its light, sending out a ray of itself into experience. That ray of passion attracts energy (which is generally dualistic, meaning it has a positive [+] and negative [-] expression) and ultimately manifests reality. Then you, as a souled being, leap into the new reality for experience. Not for lessons, not for atonement, but for the joy of living within your creation.

The passion of the soul will sometimes override the human needs and desires, because it doesn't really understand them. You've been playing the human game – caught up in needs rather than passion, thoughts rather than senses – and, at a certain point, the soul does supersede the human. It's not really intervening; it's just taking its own course and doesn't care if the human comes kicking or screaming or dead, because that simply doesn't make a difference to the soul.

That's why awakening can be so difficult. The soul is ready to move and the human says, "Why is all this bad stuff happening in my life?" You look to astrology charts and tarot readings and all that, but it's simply because the soul, in its sensual love for self, is moving on. It tires of its own human games and moves on.

Maybe you say, "Well, that's brutal. Doesn't the soul understand that I don't want to get cancer? That I don't want to lose my house?" No, it really doesn't, because those are fleeting experiences of the human. At a certain point, the soul, which is you, doesn't want to keep getting caught up in the human minutia. It loves the human self, but it's more interested in the experience of existence rather than the experience of limitation.

So there is an interesting dynamic going on and it might almost get you angry. "What?! Don't I have a say in this whole thing?!" Ah, that's where we bring it all together. You absolutely do. You absolutely *can* work on the level of soul *and* human to choose not only how you want to walk through your experience – how it will build, how it will unfold – but also how you will realize it and how you will experience in the future. It's amazing!

Ah, take a deep breath.

You've gone through a lot of information and energy here; now take a moment to really feel into it all – the I Am with its wisdom, with its passion to feel itself; the human with its needs, with its rich experiences. Feel into this sacred, critical juncture of realization while embodied; the realization of the I Am, the soul passion, while also fulfilling the human needs.

Take a deep breath and feel.

The soul's passion is immeasurable. It doesn't change or fluctuate. It is constant, always there, always prevailing. And it's what you have connected to in your darkest moments and altered states. But you don't need to have these extreme experiences to feel the passion of your soul. You can do it right now.

It's not necessarily a heartbeat or a rhythm, not even what you call light or love. It's simpler than that. The passion of your soul is less defined than any of that.

Take a deep breath and feel the passion of your soul.

Human has Needs and Desires

While the divine has passion, the human has needs and desires.

In fact, the human has a *lot* of needs and that's perfectly acceptable. Living in this human reality, you have material needs for food, air, water and shelter. You have emotional needs for love, companionship and acceptance. In fact, probably the biggest of all the emotional needs, even more than love, is to be accepted. Why? Because you have a hard time accepting yourself, so you go outside for that acceptance, looking for it in other people and situations.

You try to find acceptance in your job, which is really a hard thing to do, because everybody else is trying to find it too. But who grants the acceptance? Ah, that's part of the game in the workforce; you don't really know who's giving the acceptance.

You look for acceptance in relationships. Sometimes you might call it love, but usually it's really looking for acceptance. Yes, there are cases of real love, but so much of a relationship is about acceptance and reflectance – reflecting you off your partner; using your partner to fill certain voids within you; or just looking to see if your partner is accepting you so that you can accept yourself.

The human needs money. It's a pretty important factor of surviving in today's society, but so often it's a challenge for so-called spiritual people to actually admit they need money, let alone receive and accept abundance for themselves.

You have needs for health and comfort, and these needs are important. They're not to be denied, but it's also important to make sure that the soul understands those needs.

You see, the soul doesn't have the same concern about your human needs as you do. To you, they are of utmost importance, usually placed far before the need for things like enlightenment. You can wait on enlightenment, but you can't wait too long for dinner!

Take a deep breath and really feel into your human needs for a moment. What are they? Write them down, if you wish, and get as detailed and practical as you want.

What are your human needs?

Yes, there are a lot of them. You may have a long list of your human needs, and that is perfectly acceptable. To deny your needs is to deny an important part of yourself.

Humans are focused on survival needs, as well as the deep need to validate their identity in this reality. Time and energy are used to validate this reality, and then to validate yourself within it, so you can see how easy it is to get deeply immersed in this reality due to the basic needs for validity and survival. It's rather limited, but it's part of the experience.

You have to let the soul know what you need. You say, "But doesn't the soul understand that I have a bank account, that I need a car and money?" Not really, because, in a sense, it doesn't really care. In its desire for experience the soul isn't distracted by those things. Now we're going to put them together so it truly understands the needs of the human, but not to the point where those needs overrule the true passion of the soul.

Divine is Sensual

The soul, the I Am, loves sensual, sensory experiences. It doesn't judge them, just relishes them. Whether it's through you as its human aspect or itself simply going into the deep, sensual feeling of "I exist," it loves the sensual experience. The soul loved its time expressing itself as an angel in the cosmos, out in the other dimensions; feeling itself as color, as a nonphysical being, a sort of gaseous substance. It loved feeling its identity and experiencing itself with other entities out in the realms, not to fulfill any need other than to feel; not to do anything other than to know itself, again and again. It loves the sensual, sensory experiences.

Out in the cosmos there is music, color, movement, energy, interdimensional dances. The soul loves these. The entire cosmos is the soul's playground. Every one of these sensual experiences comes back to the soul as a reminder – "I exist! Glory be to Self, I exist. I can never *not* exist, and therefore, I know not fear. I exist."

Angels, souls, are very sensual beings. They love to *feel*. They love sensory experience, whether through color, music, time travel, density or any other type of sensual experience. In fact, the desire for a sensual, sensory experience is what brought you here to Earth. Being on Earth is an amazingly sensual experience for an angelic being, because you can experience yourself in a very slow and dense reality.

This sensual nature is inherent within you. It's an integral part of you. Even as a human, you seek sensual experiences in your physical reality – sometimes distorted and twisted – but just for the sake of a sensual experience. It's often interpreted or experienced through very physical things like making love, eating food, walking in the woods, singing at the top of your lungs, seeing a scary movie, riding a roller coaster and other intense activities. It is all sensual experience and expression, and the soul *loves* that. It drinks it in deeply.

Feel into that for a moment. Feel the soul self and its brilliant desire for sensual experience.

Human is Emotional

In contrast to the very sensual nature of the soul, the human has thought and emotion. The human mind likes to think it feels, but it really can't have true sensory feelings, so it created a false sensory nature – false, because it's not truly sensual – called emotion. Then the human mind finds ways to create emotion and drama as a cheap substitute for true sensual experience. The mind believes it is feeling, but it's really just having emotions. And to many humans, even the words 'emotion' and 'feeling' are interchangeable.

You know someone (maybe even yourself) who, when things are stable and going along fine in their life, always seems to find a way to totally mess it up, disrupt everything and bring in drama. You know people who always have drama around them – drama with their families, drama in their thoughts, something always crashing down so they can go in and rescue others or have somebody rescue them. It somehow helps them feel alive, but it's all based on thought rather than on truly sensual experience.

Imagine for a moment that you actually let go of the drama and emotions. At first, it may seem rather boring. You kind of miss it, because those were feeding troughs for you. They were places where you got energy and had energy taken from you.

But imagine transcending this thought/emotion pattern and allowing true sensual experience into your life. The type where, for instance, you go into the ocean or a swimming pool, where you're immersed in water; and it's not just feeling the cold wet against your skin, but where the water is alive and your skin is interacting with it; and you're breathing in the essence of the water, not into your lungs, but the energetic essence into your self. That's where it becomes a true experience, animated and full of life. *That* is a sensual experience! Most of the time you get into the water only to bathe or cool off or relax for a few minutes, but never get intimately into the *experience* of the water.

You could say that about anything. Consider artwork. A lot of times the eye sees the artwork on the wall and says, "Well, that's nice." You like it or don't like it. But in the true sensual experience, that art comes to life and you're suddenly within it and experiencing it. It's alive and you're interacting with it. There's no emotion or drama, no judgment of "I like this; I don't like that." It is simply a deep, sensual experience.

This is where you're going as an embodied Master in this new era. This is what life becomes – a very, very sensual experience.

Divine loves Experience

Your divinity doesn't really understand things like human pain and suffering or not having enough money. To the divinity, it's just an experience. There is no judgment about whether it's good or bad. But the human, of course, feels the suffering.

The soul loves experience. It is not afraid of anything, anyone or of any experience. It's not afraid of too much energy. Sometimes you have a difficult time in a place of high or chaotic energy and it overwhelms the body. But in a true experience of the soul, there is no overwhelm. There is no such thing as 'too much.' There is nothing that needs to be filtered out. You can open up and dive into pure sensual experience without fear, without worry about burning out your body or offending other people or having the wrong result. You just have a full-on sensual experience.

The soul has the magnificent, immense sense of the *I Am, I Exist*, then it dives into a beautiful, simple and nonjudgmental experience of sensuality. To the soul there is no right or wrong kind of incident; it is just falling in love with Self again and again through every new sensual experience.

Human loves Action

While the divine bathes in experience, the human likes to take action. It likes to act upon, react to and force energy, as well as have goals, plans and programs, all of which are very mental. The human self wants a cause and an effect. It wants to move energy and *feel* that it's moving energy. Of course, in reality, the energy is going to move anyway, but the human likes to take charge of it – or at least think it's in charge.

Along with human action comes drama – lots and lots of drama! Drama provides stimulation, and in an odd way it reminds the human that they are alive. That's why so often, when someone's life is calm and balanced, they create drama to "stir the pot" as a way of (falsely) feeling that they are alive. Oh, humans do the craziest things!

Even when taking action or having drama, the human doesn't usually feel the whole experience. The mind blocks out most of what is actually happening in any experience and says, "I don't see it or hear it, so it's not happening." But you can actually go back to a past experience and feel what *really* happened, because there was so much more to it. Yet the mind segments it and judges it, only remembering the traumatic parts, and then it continues to play that tape over and over.

Then, to make it even more confusing, the human tries to process that event. They want to understand it and heal it, so they go to a psychologist and talk about it, reliving it over and over. But that only continues to validate the very limited nature of the experience, making it even more locked in.

The human plans and plots the actions that it will take. Even in your own enlightenment you've been trying to take action, but why? The soul is going to handle your enlightenment. All you have to do is receive it, allow it, and experience it. But the human still thinks it has to plan things out, that it has to take a certain action in order to have a certain result.

Now, this is not to demean the human. I'm simply pointing out how you've been operating, acting and reacting and, eventually, how to put it all together. We're not going to eliminate the human; we're going to integrate divine and human. We're going to integrate passions *and* needs, because they're both important.

Take a deep breath and feel into what that would be like – an open, sensual, passionate, playful, raw, fully feeling experience.

Divine has Radiance

The soul just loves going through its passionate, sensual experiences. Many of the higher consciousness entities on the other side, especially if they've been to Earth, will create a special dream state, one that's very real to them – a room, an amazing outdoor scene, an elaborate meal, or anything else they want – just to have that sensual experience.

When the being then goes through this passionate sensual experience there is a burst of radiance from the soul. You could say it's like light, but it's even more refined than that. It's an opening, a brilliance. It is once again the realization, once again the falling in love with itself. Each time the soul has a sensual, beautiful experience there is another level and layer of radiance, of opening, of falling in love with itself. Ah, very beautiful.

Feel into that for a moment, the amazing radiance of the soul. When you the human goes through a passionate sensual experience – whether you deem it bad or good – the soul just drinks it in and radiates, illuminating itself all over again.

It continues to open and expand with every new experience. The soul has no judgment whatsoever, no wish that something had been done differently. The soul simply loves its life, its existence, its Self and every single experience it ever has.

Human has Judgment

After the human goes through its actions and experiences, it judges– "Was that good or bad? Did I like it or not like it? Did it turn out right or wrong?" You'll never find the soul doing that. To the soul, it is just an experience. The human worries about poverty and the future and dying. The soul doesn't worry about a thing. The human mind makes a lot of judgments, which become energetic imprints that are stored in the memory and used later for reference when you're considering your next action or going through your next experience.

The mind is very relational. In other words, it relates every event and every experience to something in the past. It relates everything you do to something you've already done. When you have a decision or a choice to make, the mind instantly correlates it to something that's happened in the past. Even if it isn't exactly the same, the mind will try to find something that was relatively close, because it is relational.

Those relational judgments eventually become limitations to the soul's experiences. The more actions and experiences you go through, the more judgments are contained in the mind's database and the more limited it becomes. Then it gets harder to make a decision and pretty soon you're in the same old rut doing the same old thing, thinking it's safe since you know the outcome before you ever really start. The more lifetimes and experiences you've had on Earth, the more judgmental and limited you become, because now you have a whole history of trying to determine what's right and wrong, good and bad, what you like or dislike. So, because of the mind's relational judgment, you get into a very repetitive mode, playing out the same types of scenarios over and over again.

Eventually, something comes up that says, "I am so sick of this repetition. I'm sick of this daily grind, doing the same thing over and over." Something screams out within you, "We've got to do something different!" But then, when the question comes up, "Hey, do you want to step over the threshold of enlightenment *right now?*" – woops! – you pull back. "Any day now, just not today."

No matter what kind of experience you have, no matter what judgment the mind has put on it, the soul takes the sensual experience and distills it into a beautiful drop of wisdom that flows right back into the soul.

The symbol of wisdom is the chalice, representing the soul accepting the wisdom of all its experiences.

As a matter of fact, right now, while you're sitting here reading these words, all the experiences that you're having as a human are being distilled by the soul into wisdom. Soul doesn't care about details, dates, times or even your value judgments. It takes each sensual experience and distills it into a drop of wisdom that's placed back into the soul, and the process starts all over again – the soul drinking in the love of itself, drinking in the joyous feeling and knowingness that it exists. Beautiful!

By contrast, the mind will take its judgment, store it in memory and define that as reality. Worse yet, the mind has a distorted view of what happened in the past and therefore a distorted view of its current reality.

Let's say an incident happened to you three days ago. The mind will remember the more dramatic portions of the event, ignore the less obvious portions, and then tell itself – and believe itself – that certain things happened in a certain pattern on a certain date. It is absolutely not true, but the mind believes it and says, "Well, no. I remember. It was 12:07 when my car hit another car and that's exactly what happened." No, that's all you *remember* of what happened. You didn't notice all the other energies and experiences that surrounded that event and therefore it became a trauma point for the human.

You store that perceived event in your memory, it becomes part of your false past, is then used to determine where you're going – or think you're going – in the future, and suddenly it has become a limitation. The more lifetimes and experiences you have, the more limitations and restrictions you install. Pretty soon, you find yourself saying, "I'm never going to leave the house again, because all these bad things happened every time I went out." That's the way the mind works. A bit dramatized, of course, but that's the way it works.

Memory is important, as long as it's *true* memory and not just a limited perspective of what you think happened.

Judgments – you could do with a lot less of them. On the other hand, they can also be what I call sensual judgments. Rather than hard, tightly defined duality judgments, they can be more like, "This experience was *way* cool; that experience was okay." You can even integrate judgment, so it's more of a feeling and not so black and white – "I like that; I'll try this again; that's not my favorite thing to do."

As we integrate soul radiance and human judgment together, obviously the human will need to take action at times. That's why you have a body and live in a linear reality. Action is important, but let it be action that brings real experience rather than action that brings limitation; action not for the sake of cause and effect, but action for the sake of experience.

The mind and thoughts are somewhat important, but as you go beyond the limitations of the mind, you'll get into the intuition, the sensual nature of things, the open, non-linear divine intelligence. Perhaps you have felt things like vertigo or dizziness. It is because you are starting to operate in the sensual intuitive knowingness mode rather than the thinking mode.

Divine has Wisdom
The divine distills every experience into wisdom.

The soul strips away all the facts and figures of its experiences – the dates, the lifetimes, the identities, the details – because they don't matter. They are nonessential. The soul takes the essence of it all and distills it into pure wisdom.

The wisdom is so simple that you can't even define it. I see it like a golden drop of honey, so sweet is this wisdom! The soul takes every experience of every human lifetime and aspect, squeezes out everything nonessential, and comes up with this beautiful luminous drop of pure wisdom.

Then the soul drinks that in. It brings the essence back to itself in the purest state, the wisdom that's been derived from the sensual experiences, and drinks it in. Then it falls in love with itself once again. Ah, it is so sweet!

The soul wants to experience just for the sake of experiencing. It doesn't need to validate itself for it is already complete in the knowing that "I Exist."

Everything that you've ever done, experienced, or thought is distilled by *You*, dear souled being, into pure wisdom. And then You, the soul, fall in love with yourself again and again.

The human might wonder if this ever gets boring for the soul. Not at all! It's the true experience of "I exist. I Am that I Am." And the soul smiles, radiant, because it knows it is already complete.

The soul knows it's going through many amazing experiences through its human self, and it will distill everything down to its pure essence. The soul is so beyond all the wounds and the garbage and the thinking. It just distills all of its Self into wisdom.

It is so simple.

The funny thing is that you already know this; you've already realized it. It's like déjà vu. I know you've already sat here with me talking to you and you letting yourself feel this. That's why it's so familiar. It's what you already know, what you have already sensed, but perhaps the human self has forgotten.

Human has Memories

The human side to the soul's wisdom is memory. Intellect. Details. The mind stores details and emotions in its memory vault with all the little facts and figures it can possibly remember. It stores it all and says, "I'm going to pull this up and use it later when I need it."

The fallacy is that the mind is actually not a very good database. Because of its judgment, it puts things in memory with a lot of bias and judgment. It remembers some of the details, but forgets a lot of them, and some it will even change.

You think about your life with your mind. You even think about your spirituality and enlightenment with your mind. But what if you allowed your divine to come through, so that, instead of thinking from a limited mental perspective, you were actually feeling into the soul passion? Instead of being tossed about by your emotions, what if you allowed yourself the sensual feeling? Instead of judging your actions and storing them in memory, what if you allowed yourself to enjoy *every* experience, and then distill the wisdom into every part of you?

What if you allowed your human and divine to finally come together in the greatest love and compassion?

DIVINE	HUMAN
Passion	Needs and Desires
Sensuality	Emotions
Experience	Action
Radiance	Judgment
Wisdom	Memories

~ 9 ~

Reunion

I Am.
I Exist.
I don't ask how I came into existence, for I have always been.
In my awakening from the human condition, I realized that I wasn't going to any place in particular. I wasn't trying to reach a point somewhere in the future, because I realized that all the points were coming to me. I no longer looked forward into time, but allowed time to come to me. I realized that I was multidimensional.
I exist.
I exist; therefore all things are possible.
I exist – a miracle.
I exist and I always will.

* * *

What if all of the points that you would normally perceive to be in your future are really in the Now? What if it was all happening right now? What if now was not just a single, potentially life-changing event, but many events simultaneously? In your awakening, you realize how multidimensional you are. There's no longer a future or a past. There is only the Now.

The mind cannot possibly understand the Now, because the Now just left. The mind tries to hold on to the Now, but it cannot. The I Am, the essence, knows nothing *but* the Now. It is always present. That's why the soul really doesn't understand what you call your past. It finds the past to be an odd concept. Neither does the soul really understand this thing you call the future – especially worry about the future – because it only knows the Now moment. It only knows "I Exist" in the Now.

"Now" is a feeling. It is an experience. It cannot be defined or understood or recreated by the mind. The mind will try to manufacture its false imitation of the Now moment and you'll tell yourself, "I'm in the Now." But there is no Now that you can know of. Only the soul, the I Am, can feel and understand and distill the Now.

The mind tries to understand the soul, but it can only relate to the soul as a grander, mystical human. The soul does not think like a human and, in a strange, way it cannot even relate to the human journey because the human is limited and the soul is limitless. But you, the human, can allow yourself to *feel* your soul, without thinking or expectation, and thus begin a new relationship with who you really are.

An Experience
For the next few minutes, allow yourself to let go of distractions and open your feelings.

Now, in this precious Now moment, let's bring the soul and the human together.

Allow yourself to go back and forth, feeling a song from human to soul and then a song back from soul to human. You don't necessarily use words, but feel into the needs of you, the human. The basic needs in your everyday life – money, a car, a house, any of that.

And then, human, listen; feel the passion of the soul, the sensual nature of the soul, the desire of the soul to have unfettered expression. Feel, human, into the soul's loving desire for experience and then the radiance, the glow that the experience brings to the soul. It cannot be felt by the human if the human is suppressing or limiting or overmanaging this beautiful radiance.

Feel, as the soul distills all of the details of your experience, strips it of all of its mentalness and distills it into beautiful wisdom to drink back into itself.

And, dear soul, listen to the human – the human who takes action, who has a body, who discerns likes and dislikes. Listen, as the human puts things into memory, because, soul, even though you don't have a memory, there's something beautiful about that human memory. You can remember and feel back into something that happened before. Dear soul, you haven't had that beautiful experience of going into your memories and remembering something precious, beautiful, amazing.

Soul and human, sing to each other, hear each other, feel each other.

Oh, you are of the same essence, but it's been a long time since you've been in the same moment, in the same experience.

One being, two separate experiences, in this beautiful sacred space. Let your humanness sing out to your soul. Let your soul sing to the human.

What are your needs, human? What do you need in order to stay here on this planet in this body? What are *your* needs that aren't about other people?

Let your soul know. Be clear. Let it know.

For you to stay present and joyful, what are your needs?

Let yourself sing out to your soul. Not begging, just letting yourself be heard.

Do you need health? Abundance? A good night's sleep? The ability to process food so you can enjoy it without gaining weight? The soul doesn't understand being overweight, but the human does. It can be challenging and take away from your comfort, your self-worth.

Let the soul know that this is no longer acceptable.

Sing out to your soul in joy, in knowingness, in clarity.

Imagine that you are packing for the next part of your journey and experience here on this planet in the physical body. You can bring anything you want, anything you need. You have had a lot of experience in this thing called life, and you can take anything you want into this next phase. Don't hold back. It can be physical, emotional, anything you want. It can be self-worth, self-love, clarity, efficiency, ease, all of these things. It can be very literal – a car, a house, money – whatever it takes to realize your dreams. There are no barriers, nothing holding you back other than your own beliefs and limits.

Tell your I Am, "Dear soul, you really haven't had the experience like I have here on this planet. Here's what we're going to need. Here's what I choose. Here's what we bring. Oh yes, we can make changes along the way. We can adapt and adjust, let some things go, bring new things in, but we're going to be starting a new phase of our journey now. Here's what we're going to bring." It can be a good body, abundance, self-love, clarity – whatever you choose; put it in that suitcase.

Your soul, your I Am also it has its desires. It has a desire and a passion for sensual experience and that passion can never be extinguished.

The human actually has limited its sensory experience because it got painful at times, but the soul still has this intense desire for very sensual experiences. The soul wants to feel the colors, hear the music, play with the energies. It's all about the senses.

The soul allows every experience. It doesn't control or limit them. And, as it comes into this reality to join with you, it's asking you to understand – understand the soul, understand its desires, understand its ways.

So, dear soul, sing to the human – your precious human self. Let it feel what you desire.

Dear soul, sing clearly to the human so it can know and feel you.

Now, as they come together, feel that magic dance between the human and the divine, a dance that brings together what has been apart for a very, very long time. The dance of divine and human – the needs and the passions; the sensual nature and the mind; the memories and the distillation; the wisdom – all coming together.

Feel the dance of human and divine, each greeting and welcoming the other, embracing, feeling each other, dancing, melding into each other, exploring each other.

Take a good deep breath in this moment.
Feel free to stand up. Let yourself move with the energies.
Let yourself feel.
Let the divine feel the human body as it moves.
Let the divine hear the song of your human.
   Ah, it is times like this that I long to be back in the physical body to be with you.

III

SPIRITUAL PHYSICS

~ 10 ~

How Energy Works

Now, let's talk about how energy works, because it's an important part of understanding the act of consciousness.

Everything starts with consciousness. The circumpunct, a circled dot, is an ancient symbol that represents consciousness – your consciousness. It also represents your soul, because your divine is pure consciousness. The dot in the center represents your origin from All That Was, also known as Source or God; the outer circle represents all the experiences your soul has ever had.

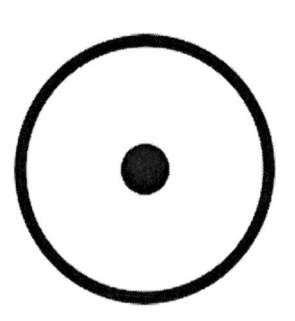

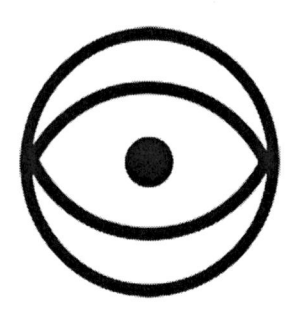

As you have your experiences and your soul distills them, the essence comes back into the soul as wisdom, so we draw the circumpunct with the sacred, all-seeing eye representing the wisdom, the knowingness that is within you right now. It is that wisdom and knowingness that brought about your awakening.

Feel into that and you'll have the essence of mastery, of energy, of enlightenment. Follow that inner knowingness; it will be the greatest guiding light you'll ever have.

Consciousness, represented by the circumpunct, contains no energy whatsoever. None.

The question is: where did energy come from? If there is no energy in consciousness, if Spirit is not energy, where did energy come from?

Energy came from passion. It was generated from the tremendous passion of the soul when that first question arose, "Who am I?" It came from the passion that felt, "I Exist!"

In the beginning, energy did not exist. There was nothing but consciousness. The consciousness felt a passion rise up within, a passion to exist, to know the I Am, to experience itself. That passion of consciousness was so intense, so fierce that it compressed and condensed the edge of consciousness, and this created energy. You could say that, at the very boundary of consciousness, your soul created such a desire and a tension that it compressed and condensed consciousness into energy. It was the original transmutation – changing consciousness into energy.

It was a beautiful, amazing thing. *Energy is crystallized, compressed consciousness.* It was created by you, for you, in order to have your experiences. It was brilliant, having that level of passion – "I Am! I Exist!" It has been done only once, and that initial expression created all energy, which is the tool or vehicle that you would use from then on to create your experience.

It was brilliant, because it left the soul pure. In a way, the energy went outside of consciousness in order to always leave consciousness untainted. Nothing will ever distort, pollute or tarnish your soul.

You can have grand experiences, from the lightest of the light to the darkest of the dark, and still never alter the purity of your consciousness. That profound truth nearly brings me to tears. To have that depth of passion which created an energy that would never corrupt the soul – it is absolutely beautiful.

That passion of consciousness created all of the energy that you still use today.

* * *

Now, let's discuss the different levels and layers of energy, keeping in mind here that passion created energy.

You are a souled being; a being of consciousness, surrounded by energy.

There are four basic levels of energy.

Level 1 – Core

The first level, the one that is closest to you, is called your *Core energy*. It's always been the same quantity of energy and it is only yours. It can never be taken by anybody or harmed by anything. It is *your* Core energy, your own personal energy, and it can never be mixed or intermingled with the energy of another souled being.

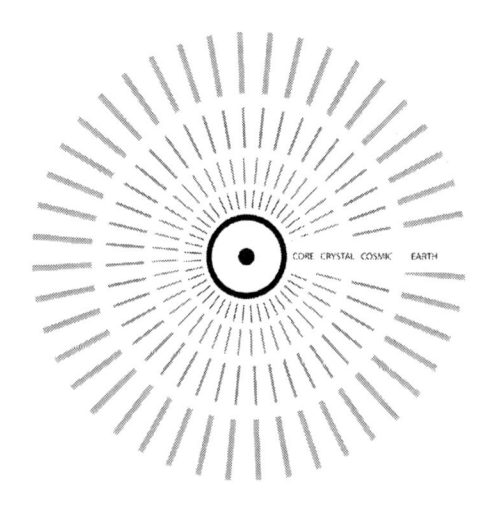

For the most part, because it is so close to you, you aren't even aware of Core energy, but it's always there. It has no mass. It has no color. It is absolutely clear and pure. It never changes. You can't give it away to anyone else and nothing can pollute it. This Core energy is absolutely yours and it is the closest thing there is to divine passion.

Level 2 – Crystal

The next level is called *Crystal energy*. Crystal energy was created the moment you encountered other souled beings; when you brought your Self, your awareness, to theirs. That melding and bringing together of souled beings created this next level called Crystal energy. It's very, very pure, but it took two or more beings of consciousness coming together to create this level.

Once again, it's something that you rarely access or use. It's a very beautiful and refined energy, but, because it's not exclusively yours, it doesn't have the same level of purity as your Core energy.

The Crystal energy is a wonderful energy to tap into, particularly when working with other people. If you're a healer or a facilitator, doing a group project or somehow working with others, tap into this Crystal level of energy. It will bring a whole new level of clarity and passion to your co-creation.

Crystal energy is always present. It is all around you right now. It's a very strong energy and it changes. It has a variance as the strength fluctuates from time to time.

This Crystal energy is one of the reasons why people come back together in groups, again and again. They're warriors in one lifetime, together as a family in the next, because there is a Crystal energy for that group. Eventually it may turn into karma and all sorts of other things, but Crystal energy created by a group can stay intact for a long, long time. Your family has its own type of Crystal energy to it.

Level 3 – Cosmic

The next level is *Cosmic energy*. Cosmic energies are the first energies that start coming into physical reality, into your physical universe and into some of the surrounding dimensions. These energies have much more density than Core or Crystalline energies. Cosmic energies are the building blocks of this universe. They allow for you to have things like time, space and matter.

Cosmic energies can go in and out of this very dense, physical Earthly reality, as can the Crystal energies (but not Core energies). In other words, Cosmic and Crystal energies are accessible to you right here on Earth.

Humans do not generally tap into Cosmic energies, but they are sometimes used by other beings around the cosmos. Cosmic energies are wonderful to use for things like space travel, and for overcoming some of the material obstacles of things like gravity and other physical forces.

Cosmic energies can be very important when you start becoming aware and operating in multiple realities at one time, because these other realities don't necessarily utilize Earth energies. The Cosmic energies can be tapped into in your multidimensional realities whether you go out on a journey or experience a multidimensional reality right here.

Level 4 – Earth

Finally, we have the Earth energies, the ones used by humans in this reality. These are the energies that create matter and your Earth physics and sciences. They are pretty much what everybody uses all the time. Earth energies are very dense and solid compared to the others. They don't move very fast and they are not very flexible.

These are the basic energies that you work with, but remember that all of the energies originated from soul passion.

They've been scaled down, descending and condensing level by level, but they all come from the same origin – your passion – and that should tell you something very important.

Let's talk about passion for a moment. One of the biggest challenges of enlightenment is the loss of what you called passion. But you associated human passion with something that wasn't really true passion. It was more like a strong desire. A human passion was something that kept you occupied – a hobby or an activity, a passion for gardening, a passion for doing volunteer work or for reading – and then suddenly it was gone. Bewildered, you asked, "Where's my passion?" One of the most common questions from awakening humans is, "How do I get my passion back?"

Well, you're not going to get that kind of passion back. Those "passions" were somewhat interesting preoccupations and you might have loved doing them, but they weren't your true passion.

The *real* passion is to be able to sit here as a human *and* a soul, and feel into the "I Exist. I Am." Now, you might think, "Well, that's not much fun. I want a passion to do something. I want something that makes me happy when I get up in the morning, something to get me through the day. I want a little excitement in an otherwise dull, boring day."

But the *real* passion, and what really attracts energy, is this core passion – the "I Exist." That's the true soul passion and that's what will bring abundance, creativity, health, and everything else you desire.

I've been asked to do a class on abundance, but it's actually very simple. *Abundance is directly related to your passion for life.* When you have passion for life, abundance is there. When you have passion for life, your body responds accordingly. When you have passion for life, everything is going to be there for you.

Please remember: *passion created energy* and now it is passion that attracts energy.

You may say, "I kind of get it, but where do I find this passion? How do I bring it up from within me?" Well, you can't do it by thinking about it or by repeating, "I have passion, I have passion," because there's no passion in that!

By the way, the reason thought-based manifestation techniques don't really work is that there is very little passion in thoughts. Thoughts are kind of flat without a lot of color or life in them. You can think and think and think, and there's still not much passion; therefore, not much energy.

You can go to one of these 'manifestation' or 'positive thinking' courses and get kind of excited –"Wow! Maybe I found the answer" – because you see some wealthy person up front giving the class and taking your money. You think, "Maybe I can be like that," so there is an initial blip of something like passion. A few things work out, a few synchronicities, a few nice coincidences, but then it's right back into the same old rut. Do you blame the instructor? No, you blame yourself – for something you didn't get, something you don't know – and you're right back in the old routine.

Abundance is directly related to your passion. So it brings us to a kind of critical point.

What is your passion? Where is your passion? How is your passion? It's probably kind of flat. Not bad, but kind of flat compared to where it could be. On a scale of one to ten, your passion is probably around a two, and that's all right.

A lot of your old human passion has been ripped out and stripped away from you. You have so little energy left that it's tough to try to get your passion to rise up again. You wonder how you're going to make it through the day, much less the next 20 years, much less through enlightenment. There's just not a lot of passion anymore, at least in terms of the old human kind of passion.

But there absolutely is a passion, a true passion, that's always been there. It's the passion of the I Am. You don't have to manufacture it or hype yourself into it or try to be a cheerleader for it. All you have to do is take a deep breath and feel it once again. It's right there. It always has been. The I Am has a tremendous passion and that has never changed. It's what created energy and, because you are also the I Am, you can also become aware of and feel this passion.

* * *

Everyone has the same opportunity for energy, just like everyone has the same access to sunlight. No one has more or less than anyone else. You'd like to think that some people are born wealthy or with more opportunity, but they have the same energy potential as everyone else. All humans are born equal, at least in terms of energy, and all humans are receiving energy exactly appropriate for where they are on their journey.

Most humans believe there are things they have to learn, that they're still in lesson. You're not. There are no lessons for you anymore, none whatsoever. There is nothing you have to learn, nothing that you haven't already experienced. There are a lot of things that you keep re-experiencing over and over, but it's all just an act. You keep playing it out, usually with the same ending, and then jump back in and act it out again hoping something will change. But it generally doesn't, until you say, "*No more.*"

Everyone has the same amount of energy. A person who has a lot of money is working with the same level of energy as the person who's absolutely broke. They're both dealing with the same quantity of energy, but one is applying it to the act of abundance, while the other is applying it to the act of poverty. It's not that somebody has more or less energy; it's just what their consciousness is doing with it.

Every human has not only the gift but also the right to change their act at any time and, therefore, change how energy is working for them. However, most humans do not believe they have this capability. They think they have to steal energy or power from someone else, but power actually doesn't exist. Most humans *believe* in power and believe they have to get it, but power itself is an illusion. (More about this in chapter 14.) Most humans believe they have to take something from others in order to have it for themselves, rather than recognizing that all they have to do is change their consciousness, which then changes the type and flow of energy in their life. It really is that simple, at least until you get into human belief systems, patterns, ruts, the hypnosis, mass consciousness and everything else.

Humans are highly hypnotized or programmed, not by aliens but by themselves, and they continually accept more and more programming from mass consciousness. We call it the "anything but myself" syndrome, the belief that you get it, whatever 'it' is, anywhere but from yourself.

To walk out of that programming, you simply make a choice and say, "No more." You decide that the only thoughts that really belong to you are the ones you choose and that nothing else is yours. That's how to deprogram yourself. It's all you need.

Of course, in reality, the mind will battle with you and say, "No, it must be yours, because you thought it, you've adapted to it, and you've accepted it and believed it for a long time." That's when you say, "I Am that I Am. That is *not* my thought, not my consciousness anymore," and you let it go. It really is that simple.

~ 11 ~

Consciousness

Everything comes from consciousness. Energy was born from the passion of your consciousness. You could say that *energy is passionated consciousness*.

Soul passion is deep, subtle, oh so still, but yet so very rich. Ah! It is a beautiful feeling.

The passion of the soul will never go away. At times you'll be more aware of it than at other times, but it's always there. It's truly a feeling beyond words.

Your soul passion – the "I Am, I Exist" – created energy, because it wanted to experience itself in every way possible. It wanted to live within its creation. It wanted to experience the expansion, the contraction and everything in between.

Energy, created from soul passion, responds to the act of consciousness, the expression of consciousness. That means no matter what you're doing or how you're acting, energy is *always* responding. Energy is very literal and it responds literally to your act, to what you're *ac*tually putting out, and manifests that into your life. When the act changes, the alignment of energy changes and responds accordingly.

Even if you think you're just faking it or making it up, energy still responds accordingly. Pretend you're an actor on a stage, acting out whatever you want, and notice how the energy changes, because it is responding to the act of consciousness. Whether you're conscious of your consciousness or not, whether you're aware of your act or not, energy will always respond. If you want abundance, act abundantly. If you want health, act healthy.

Now, granted, it's going to seem a little odd at first, because you think you're just making it up. But remember, *everything* is made up! Your human life is just a temporary act, no matter how real you think it is.

Humans in general have very little understanding of consciousness. It is vastly undiscovered and unknown. With all the science and math and powerful computers, it's amazing that consciousness is still not part of the equation on this planet. Even though consciousness is at the core of creation – it actually creates creation – humans are essentially unaware of it. This should provide you with many, many clues about why the world is where it's at today, as well as the dire need for consciousness explorers, engineers and scientists. Perhaps, just perhaps, this is work that *you* will undertake, because you understand consciousness more than most other humans.

It's interesting that very few people talk about the origins of energy, much less the origins of consciousness. In fact, it amazes me, because this is one of the most fundamental dynamics in the omniverse, yet most people go about their everyday life without ever giving it a single thought.

Most people will never feel into the intimacy and passion of the "I Am, I Exist." Even religious and New Age groups don't understand the very simple principles of consciousness and energy because they're busy worshipping distractions such as gods, angels, saints, spirit guides, healing modalities and energy alignment devices. I call this makyo – or spiritual distraction – because without the basic, intuitive understanding of consciousness and energy, these things fail to bring you to the *feeling* of the deep passion of the soul and consciousness. And without that deep feeling, it's nothing but mental and philosophical distraction.

You cannot have life without consciousness. Trees, birds, water, flowers, dogs, music, food, even thoughts would not exist if it were not for consciousness. Consciousness is at the core of everything, yet it is essentially unknown to man.

Of all the scientific facts and information, of all the history of humankind and all the research that's ever been done in space and the oceans and microbiology and everything else, there is still no accounting for this thing called consciousness. When the scientists study the universe, the cosmos, the origins of creation, there is no reference to consciousness. The religious types use a reference to God, the New Agers will reference Spirit, but there is little or no reference to the role of consciousness. Even modern psychology doesn't really acknowledge consciousness. They account for memory, thoughts and emotions, but not for consciousness.

When humans begin to understand consciousness, not in religious or intellectual terms, but rather as the core essence of all creation, humanity will make a huge leap in its evolution.

The understanding of consciousness will end wars, stop famine, negate brutal competition and bring harmony to this planet.

In these next few years, the role of consciousness will start coming to the forefront. You'll begin seeing the word "consciousness" in the news media and Internet articles, and there will be a lot of misunderstanding about it, a lot of speculation. They're going to try to dissect it and define it, and the interesting thing about consciousness is that it is very, very hard to define. But at least they will begin to acknowledge it.

Feel into this word "consciousness" for a moment.

Consciousness.

What is it?

Consciousness is awareness.

To be aware of awareness, to be conscious of your consciousness, is a huge step. "I Am, I Exist" is the simplest yet the most profound form of consciousness.

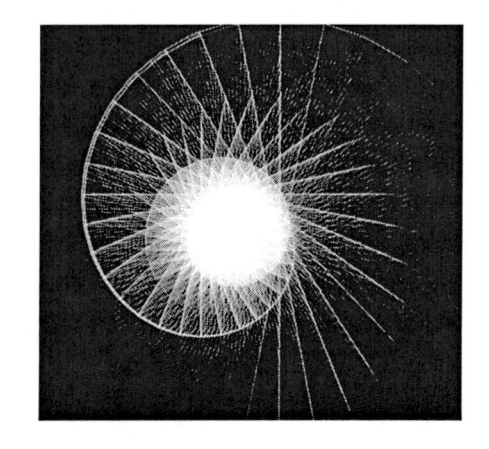

Consciousness is like a spiral, always expanding but always coming back to a reference point. Imagine it as a three-dimensional spiral. As your consciousness expands, it goes into a spiral. With each evolution it comes back to the simplicity, but yet in an expanded form. Each time the consciousness comes around again, it comes back to the simplicity of "I Exist," but now more expanded and full than ever before. Then it expands once again, going further into experience and deeper into truth and love of itself.

Consciousness is awareness. It is not thought, and that's one of the stumbling blocks in understanding it. Even those who are studying consciousness on a more academic level right now tend to equate it with intelligence and thought, and it has nothing to do with that. When they begin to comprehend the *difference* between consciousness and thought, they'll start making some quantum leaps in understanding. They'll begin to understand the "missing" ninety-five percent of matter and energy, and what's in the space between the particles.

What *is* in the space between particles? That "space" is filled with un-activated, dormant energy; energy that's sitting in neutral. But they don't recognize it yet, because they don't have the proper instruments, and they don't understand the role of consciousness in creation.

Your body is made up of cells, molecules, atoms and particles, but, even at the subatomic level, there is still tremendous space between each particle. If the nucleus of each atom was the size of a pinhead, there would be hundreds of kilometers between each one.

The vast space between particles is filled with neutral energy just waiting to respond to the act of consciousness. It's a reservoir of energy so grand that the energy in this book could provide the power for all people of a big city for the next 50 years and still have a tremendous amount left over. There is an astounding amount of energy just waiting to be activated by consciousness.

Scientists are only aware of about five percent of all matter and energy in the universe. It's actually a lot less than that, but science itself accepts it as fact that only about five percent of the total amount of matter and energy is known.

Twenty-six percent of all matter in the universe is considered "dark matter." In other words, they can't define it, they don't know what it is and they don't understand what's going on.

Roughly sixty-eight percent of all known energy is "dark energy," again because they simply don't understand what it is. It can't be measured or quantified by science, so it's just thrown into a mysterious bucket called 'dark energy.'

In other words, more than ninety-five percent of energy and matter is a mystery. Science acknowledges that something is out there, but they don't know what it is or how it works. They put labels on it such as 'dark matter' and 'dark energy,' but they basically just don't know what it is. *(Note: the above data can be found on the official NASA website.)*

It's somewhat overwhelming and potentially frightening to know there's that much energy in a dormant state. What if the bad guys got hold of it? Perhaps humans would blow up the planet very, very quickly. What if you got hold of it and made one little mistake? Boom! Yes, there is an underlying fear of all of that energy.

If you're like most humans right now, energy just barely trickles into your life. You scarcely bring in what you need; never too much, just barely enough to get by.

Society is hypnotized to have "just enough." Barely enough. In ancient times, the rulers learned that it's not really effective to starve and beat the slaves. You have to give them just enough to keep them going until the next day. Give them a little bit of pleasure, a little 'hit' of energy, and they'll keep working like zombies. A little beer, a little pizza, a little football, and they'll work hard just to get another little shot of pleasure tomorrow.

There is a tremendous amount of un-activated energy in every single breath you take, an ocean of energy just waiting for the act of consciousness, but you haven't been so sure you really like the old act. Why bring in a lot more energy just to make that old act of limitation and poor health even more intense? Why bring in more energy just to get more lack of abundance, more lack of good relationships? So you turn the energy valve down to get "just enough."

That's why, when we delve into some of these topics, it's a little frightening, because it brings up ghosts and monsters and demons. You have an inner knowingness that there is a tremendous amount of energy available and it doesn't take a lot to get it going. In fact, it only takes consciousness and awareness. But are you ready for it?

This is one thing the Merlin deeply understands: no rules, for they limit the self. There are no rules out here, in these mass multiple dimensions. *There are no rules.* There are no rules about gravity, no rules about force, no rules about duality or any of those other things. It is all free and clear, and now you, as a Master in the New Energy, can go play.

These concepts are very simple. There may be a tendency to try to over-think them, to try to create the rules around them. But, in the end, the Master understands there truly are no rules.

There is Self.

There is Experience.

And there is Expression.

Let us take a deep breath together.

As you have been reading these words, a tremendous amount of consciousness has come through you. Some of it your eyes have seen, much of it has been conveyed to you at many different levels. So, as we come to the end of this portion of the Master's Guide to the New Energy, let yourself play with what has been discussed. Let yourself experience the new Unknown.

~ 12 ~

Consciousness and Thought

Now let's discuss the difference between consciousness and thought. Consciousness is awareness, and to expand it is to be conscious of the consciousness.

Start with feeling. It's that first thing that comes to you, that first awareness.

Thought, on the other hand, is evaluation and measurement.

Now, I'm not saying thought is wrong, and soon you'll see how consciousness and thought working together is an amazing team. At some point, there will no longer be a hard line between thought and consciousness, because you'll be going back and forth.

Consciousness, like a spiral, can ebb in and ebb out. It can flow up or down, inward and outward. Consciousness expands in all directions. Actually, consciousness expands without need of direction. It simply expands. This may be a little hard for the mind to embrace, but you can feel it, if you take a moment.

Remember, I said that the soul distills everything it's ever experienced through its aspects, and brings that essence back into itself as wisdom. This wisdom is what's expanding the consciousness.

The hardest part about explaining consciousness is that I should really stop at the word "awareness." How do you describe consciousness? It's just awareness.

Thought is much easier to describe. Thought is linear instead of expansive. Human thought goes historically, chronologically, small to large, large to small. It is very, very linear. Human mind thought by itself will never be expansive like consciousness is. Thought will always be relatively linear. In thought, there is a penchant for details, facts and figures. Consciousness doesn't need any of that.

I'll give you an example of consciousness. Again, it is very, very difficult to explain, but at some point you just start feeling it. You start being aware of the awareness.

Beauty. Feel into that for a moment.

There is a resonance in the word "beauty."

I could have said, "Feel into a beautiful flower with its ivory colored petals and its beautiful green stem and its graceful presence," but those were thoughts, definitions and measurements. There may be a tinge of consciousness, but definitions like "green, ivory and petals" are primarily thoughts.

There are thoughts or words that provoke certain emotional feelings of "I like that" or "I don't like that," but those are all still coming from a thought base. When I say "beauty" without further definition, can you feel the difference?

It is more a feeling of consciousness, even though I had to use the word "beauty" just to trigger something.

Thought has to be constructive. In other words, it has to have its structures and its details. Thought is structure, design and definition, so when I talk about some 'beautiful green leaves' on the tree outside, that's a lot of definition. But if I talk about 'nature,' there's more of a resonance.

Thought knows death, finality, not just of the being, but also of itself. Thoughts know they will die, so the mind has an inherent termination built into it. Consciousness, on the other hand, knows of no such thing. Consciousness is eternal life.

Thoughts are inherently limited, because they know they will change or be replaced by another thought or be confused by a lot of other thoughts. Thoughts know death, whereas consciousness only knows life.

Thoughts know destruction. It is built into them. Thoughts almost count on destruction, because it's happened time and time again. Thoughts disintegrate. Thought looks to nature and says, "Nature breaks down. Everything falls apart and dies in the end. There is always destruction. Anything you build will be destroyed."

The mind operates on this basis of destruction. Even though it may like building and creating, the mind knows that everything it builds will be destroyed. Do you see the futility and the limitation?

Consciousness knows none of this. There is no destruction in consciousness. It is constant creation.

When I say a word like "love," what happens? First, a feeling comes, and it is followed by thoughts.

Love. There's a consciousness, an awareness of it. Love cannot be measured or analyzed. Love can only be experienced.

But yet, you've had experiences of love that bring a lot of relational thoughts – love of a parent, maybe a love gone sour or a love that hurt you. There's an initial consciousness or awareness, but then the flood of thoughts come in.

Feel into "love" in consciousness now, without the limitation, destruction and death of thought.

Feel the consciousness of love. There's a resonance.

Consciousness tickles the senses. It can literally create a feeling in the body and even a temporary euphoria in the mind.

Consciousness is unified; thought is separate and disjointed. Let's use a movie film as an example.

Thought is like taking each individual frame of the movie, cutting it apart and pasting it up on the wall, one clip after another, and saying, "This is the movie," because it goes from each individual clip to the next. Thought focuses on one frame at a time, evaluates it and says, "There are two people kissing, a bird is in the background, and a storm is coming that's going to get them wet and make them miserable." That's thought, looking at life one frame at a time. It's very separate. It tries to put itself together, saying, "Look, we have all these thoughts, all these individual frames, so isn't this a movie? Isn't this consciousness?" No, of course not.

Think of a movie you've seen recently. You probably don't remember a lot of thoughts or individual specific things about that movie, but there's a consciousness to it.

Take a deep breath and feel into the consciousness of the movie; not cut up into frames or individual moments, but the whole thing. Feel the essence of the entire experience. That's the consciousness.

Thoughts are separate. Consciousness is always whole and complete. Always.

Consciousness cannot be incomplete. It can expand, it can grow, but it can never be incomplete. It can never be unfulfilled. Thoughts are almost always incomplete, unfulfilled, needing more, feeding off more energy.

Right now, as you sit in this moment, all the thought questions you have ever asked are out floating around somewhere trying to get answers. They're dangling out in the universe, unfulfilled. They actually make up part of that dark matter. Every unanswered intellectual thought question you've ever asked is out there trying to find its answer.

Consciousness needs no answers. It's not out there somewhere. It's not tiring you out or consuming energy. It's not searching for anything. Consciousness is complete.

Thoughts are programmed. Remember that more than ninety percent of the thoughts in your head aren't even yours. They come in from outside, but yet you allow them and accept them as your own. So many thoughts get programmed in through mass consciousness, mass hypnosis, and even just through sensing what's out there.

You are opening up, feeling more than ever, but then you assume all those new thoughts and feelings are yours. They're not. They are coming in from everywhere else, but they're not yours unless you choose them to be.

Consciousness is all yours and only yours. It can never be infiltrated with any programming or with anyone else's consciousness. You cannot commingle consciousnesses. Consciousness absolutely cannot be taken over, penetrated or taken away by anybody else. It is and always will be your own.

Consciousness is singular. It's really broad, big, wide and deep, but it's singular. It doesn't need all the separation. It doesn't need anyone other than itself, not even God.

Thoughts need answers to their constant questions.

Consciousness is just consciousness. It only needs itself.

When somebody is constantly questioning, they're not really in consciousness. They're in a massive thought experience. Everything you need to know, every answer you seek, is contained within your consciousness, in the real you, the I Am. It will be a knowingness, and you may not even know how you know, but you'll just know. That's consciousness at work.

Don't give credit to some spirit guide, angel, deity or spook. It's your consciousness that already knows it. You could say that consciousness knows everything, but that's a rather mental way of defining it. It actually doesn't need to know anything. Don't ask your consciousness how rich you were ten lifetimes ago or what country you lived in. It doesn't need to remember that, doesn't care about all the details. That type of question, wanting to fill in all the details, comes from human thought. Consciousness doesn't care. It had an experience, it was amazing, and consciousness distilled it and then fell in love with itself all over again. That's all it needs.

Time and space are based in thought. Time-space doesn't even exist unless you want it to, and then you limit yourself within it. You try to figure out time and space; you study physics and quantum mechanics and everything else. And, at the end of the day, you're even more stuck in time and space, because you're trying to figure it out from within thought.

But if you take a deep breath and choose consciousness – without definition, without thought, without structure – suddenly there is no time and space.

You could say that consciousness is *to be* and thoughts are *not to be*. To be or not to be. Consciousness or thought.

Consciousness is new; thoughts are old. Thoughts are history, including future history, because thought is very linear. The soul doesn't know history. It has no history. It distills history and details and everything else, squishes out all the unnecessary stuff and drinks in the wisdom. It's all in the Now moment.

This term 'the Now moment' has been overused, but it simply means that it's all here. Yesterday and tomorrow don't matter. Nothing happened like you thought it did. "I Am that I Am." That's all.

Beliefs are also associated with thought. A belief is a limitation, which is not bad as long as you are aware that it's just a belief. When you believe in your beliefs, that's what gets you into trouble. But if you're *aware* that it's just a belief – a tool, a toy, an act, the hat you chose to wear on your new stage of consciousness – then you are free, because you can change hats any time you want.

Consciousness is knowingness. It doesn't need beliefs, not even the belief in knowingness. It is awareness. It's the light. It's the I Am. Allow yourself to be in consciousness, allow yourself to be aware without using any words or trying to remember anything other than the I Am.

Thoughts like complexity. Consciousness always returns to simplicity, again and again and again. Consciousness expands into simplicity, always returning to the simplest form, which is "I exist." If you get in trouble out there amidst those who are still asleep, if you get in trouble with your job, your family, your health or anything else, stop for a moment. Feel into the "I exist," not as a thought, but as consciousness. "I am aware of my existence. *I exist*." It attracts the energy you need and everything is there. It's that simple.

Thoughts are a fraud. In other words, thoughts – and you – will pretend they are real, but they're not. Thoughts know they're going to change and eventually die, so they inherently know they're a fraud. So when you just *think* about something like abundance, there is an underlying suspicion of yourself from yourself. It doesn't work, because there's no real energy behind thought, then you start feeling like a liar, and then your act is no good anymore.

Consciousness simply exists. When there is an act of consciousness – not of thought but of true consciousness – it will draw in the energies to support the act without any effort whatsoever.

With all its drama and judgments of things, thought contains a tremendous amount of emotion. There is no emotion in consciousness. None whatsoever, and this is where I lose people sometimes, because they can't imagine life without emotion. They want to control emotions like a warrior would control the sword. They want to use emotions with others. They want to be emotion masters, so when I say there are no emotions in consciousness, it sounds boring.

Most people almost feel dead, because they're only in thoughts. Drama and emotions make them feel alive, at least for a few moments. Even those who claim to be on the spiritual path are sometimes really just looking for magical emotions.

Consciousness does not have emotion, but it has deep, passionate, sensual *feeling*.

Feel into your consciousness right now, without any definition other than "I Exist."

Take a good deep breath into the "I Exist," the awareness of the awareness.

I Exist. I Am that I Am.

We're not going to annihilate thought. That doesn't work and isn't necessary. The difference between thought and consciousness just needs to be understood, so you can understand where you're coming from. Are you coming from thought or from consciousness? Perhaps both.

Now, you might argue that, if it's both, then you've always been coming from consciousness. It's true that the consciousness has been there, but, coming from thought, you haven't been aware of it. What good is consciousness if you're not aware of it?

Once you're aware of the awareness, you can start doing the dance of consciousness *and* thought, because going forward as an embodied conscious Master, you will be using both. Thoughts are still wonderful, beautiful tools. Thoughts help give definition and structure when you want it, but you can be in consciousness at the same time.

When it comes to your own biases, thoughts, fears and limitations, you'll start to recognize the difference between what is a thought, which will die, and what is the real I Am, which is eternal. Then you begin moving out of fear and limitation. You'll still have thoughts and they'll still bark at you once in a while. But that's when you take a deep breath and say, "That thought will die. But *I Exist.*" Then there's no more need for this battle between the thoughts and your Self. It's simply a matter of awareness.

If you have been stuck in your mind, trying to figure it all out and make sense of everything, please hear this: *You cannot make sense of it.* And you really don't want to. You can be aware of it. You can have the feeling of it. You can have thoughts and definitions about it, but you don't need to battle with the mind anymore. Let yourself be aware of the awareness – "I Am, I Exist, I'm conscious. Now, how shall I act from this moment on?"

~ 13 ~

It Comes to You

In my enlightenment, I realized that everything comes to me. Everything. In a limited human reality, you have to go out and make it happen. There is effort. You have to seek things out. But in enlightenment, it all comes to you. It's one of those natural physics of creation. It comes to you in response to your act of consciousness. That means people, abundance and energy all come in at the exact moment they are needed, never too early and never too late.

You get to the point where you don't even think about what you need next. So often, in the human reality, you have to think ahead – "What do I need for tomorrow or next week?" But in enlightenment, whatever you need is there in the perfect quantity at the perfect time.

At first, it will amaze you – "How does this happen?" But then you'll realize that it's the true nature of reality. It was always there, you just weren't aware of it.

Even time comes to you, expanding and contracting to serve your needs. Instead of always watching the clock to see what linear time it is, you'll find that time becomes flexible to accommodate your needs and desires.

There are some who think this enlightened life is boring. It is not at all. Just because you don't have challenges or drama doesn't mean it's boring! The beautiful thing about being in this state of enlightenment is you can still have your days of drama, if you want to. It's not like all human excitement is gone forever.

Reality is not singular and it's not linear. You can have your beautiful, peaceful, wisdom-filled days of nirvana and then say, "You know, tomorrow I'd like to experience a little drama. Maybe I'll get caught in a big thunder storm." Drama is fun at times. It's exciting!

The Masters in the past, the ones who ascended prior to you, they generally never had that opportunity. When they ascended, they left the physical realms without the opportunity to experience what it was like to stay in biology. But you can, if you wish. You might have days where you take on some physical aches and pains just so you can experience what it's like to quickly heal yourself. It's truly amazing.

The great thing is that you'll never get stuck. You can go in and out, having one reality or the other, simply by choosing. That's all there is to it. You don't have to think about it. It's what I call the Yo Soy el Punto. "I am the point. I am wherever I want to be." Then the energies come in to serve you.

Human reality often seems so limited and dense, but it doesn't have to be. In your lifetime, you're going to see amazing breakthroughs in the understanding of physics. Some will call it quantum physics, but it's natural physics.

Part of the game of human life is to see reality from a very limited and linear perspective, based on time, space and matter. But all reality already exists, including all the realities that you don't perceive right now. This word "perception" is going to come back to you again and again, because life and reality are truly just a matter of perception.

Quantum scientists are already beginning to have great breakthroughs in understanding the nature of reality. For instance, a particle observed in the old consciousness was thought to move in very specific patterns and directions, and be subject to very specific causes and effects. Science is based on cause and effect, but even that is beginning to change.

Quantum scientists are beginning to see that when they observe a particle, it has a certain reaction and moves in certain ways. But when that particle is not being observed through the human senses, it will move in many ways at the same time. This is not a nebulous spiritual concept; it's being studied right now. Science is beginning to realize that it's only when the human is directly observing something that it behaves in very specific limited ways. Beyond human observation, all possibilities are real.

This should tell you something very important about reality. *Reality is based on the consciousness of the observer* or at least the observer's interpretation or expectation of reality. The reality in which you are acting is simply particles and energy responding to your awareness and perception of reality. What happens when you expand your consciousness and perceptions? Reality changes.

Don't think in terms of beliefs. Beliefs come from the mind and its limited perceptions. Beliefs are actually illusions, limitations you have placed on reality. True consciousness is not a belief. It's a perspective, it's a viewpoint, but it's not a belief. At some point you have probably tried to change a belief and perhaps found that it didn't work so well. It's because consciousness creates reality, not beliefs.

When you allow your consciousness to expand, suddenly you become aware that there is so much more to reality. Yes, science, as you know it, is real, but it's just one little facet of all reality, all of which already exists. In other words, the potential of everything that you will ever do is already there, with the exception of what happens after your enlightenment, because even the soul could not know what will happen in enlightenment. Post-enlightenment reality is free and clear, blank pages for you to create in, but that's a topic for yet another book.

Reality is much more than what humans currently perceive it to be. There's so much more happening right now. Even while you're reading this book, many, many other things are happening. Energy is shifting within you right now. Your DNA is changing. Your consciousness is changing, even though you're focused on these pages and think you're just reading words.

* * *

Right now, there are miniscule particles going in and out of your reality. A particle is something that comes from the spectrum of light and light comes from the illumination of passion. There's something we call an *ica*. It's the smallest particle that directly affects physical reality.

Ica particles are not locked into this linear 3D reality. They can easily move in and out of what you call dimensions, and they're doing it right now. They bring energies from other dimensions in anticipation of your potentials, including the potential for the realization of enlightenment. It's not just happening at one level. It's happening at many levels right now.

The ica particle comes from the light family or light spectrum, because it is frequency, and all vibration or frequency falls somewhere within the spectrum of light.

The ica is a particle and it's not a particle, very much like a photon is a both a particle and a waveform. The ica is so small that it's not detectable by any current scientific instruments and is the smallest of all particles that are affected by consciousness in this reality.

Beyond just being a particle, an ica is also what I call an attractant, because it attracts energy. By itself, it's not necessarily energy, but it attracts energy that then helps form reality. It is manifested, or brought into being, by the act of consciousness.

Remember that consciousness has very little to do with thoughts or beliefs. Consciousness isn't about what you're thinking right now, it is awareness. Consciousness is brought into your act through passion, and true passion, soul passion, is what ignites light and icas, and brings reality into being.

~ 14 ~

Power is an Illusion

At the core of all things, there is no power. There is no need for it. Power is an illusion.

Your soul has no power. It is pure consciousness, without need for power or even energy.

Power is one of the grandest illusions of all. For eons of time, it has been used for manipulation and control by angels and humans. Power is used by those who are trying to get energy from outside themselves. As you come into the consciousness of enlightenment, you become aware that power is an illusion.

Power basically means the collection, storage and application of energy, and the game of power has been played in the angelic realms almost since the beginning. Angels tried to steal energy from other angelic beings because they didn't think they had enough within themselves. They thought somebody else had the answer or the energy they needed, so they tried to take it, and this ultimately created power games.

In enlightenment, you discover that you don't need much energy and there's always an abundance of it when you do need it. You also realize that when you use energy you're not taking it from another being. You can't destroy energy. It's always there. So the need for power simply goes away, including power over yourself. You find that the need for power over your mind, power over your aspects and powering your way through life simply disappears. It's an illusion, but one to which many entities and humans are addicted. They can't seem to let go of power.

There are those who accumulate power in the form of money, control over others, goods or weapons. But the enlightened being realizes that power is a great illusion, because all energy – everything you ever need – is already there ready to serve you. It doesn't have to be coerced or manipulated. There's no need for witchcraft, black magic, intimidation or any other form of persuasion.

Power is truly an illusion. How does that feel?

I see so many humans come to this threshold of enlightenment who are still seduced by power. I can see it because it's like they're wearing a suit of armor, fighting and battling their way into enlightenment. When I ask them to take off their armor, they feel vulnerable and naked. Most have a very hard time doing it, if they even attempt it at all, because they believe power kept them safe, helped them survive and got them to this point. But still I ask them to release the illusion of power. It's not going to fit through the doorway of enlightenment, and their act of "power" consciousness will only attract others who are more than happy to play power games on them.

It's a stopping point for so many, because they feel defenseless, vulnerable and weak without their power. They shrink back from the threshold of enlightenment, go back to their everyday lives, and try to power their way through yet again, until the day comes when they are truly ready to let go of power.

Take a deep breath and let power be a thing of the past. It was part of the old experience, but, going forward, you don't need it in your life. And, when you let go of power, nobody else will be able to play power games with you.

Energy will serve you naturally and completely, if you allow it. You don't need power.

~ 15 ~

Yo Soy El Punto – I Am the Point

You are never alone.

What does that mean? For one thing, it means that there are many other kindred spirits on the same journey toward enlightenment. Never before in the history of this planet have so many people been going through awakening at the same time, so you are not alone. There are many, many others.

Each journey is very personal and unique. There is no cookie cutter template, no one way to do this, but you are not alone. There are many others with whom you can laugh together, share together, and be together on this journey.

You're never alone because, when you came into this lifetime, you knew it would be the lifetime of enlightenment – not just another lifetime, but *the* lifetime – so you called forth guidance, assistance and support.

You have angelic beings like Kuthumi, Tobias, Kryon and many, many others who are here to support you in your enlightenment. Ultimately, you are the one who will experience it, but you've called forth all these Masters to be here with you at this critical point of your journey.

More than anything, it means that your own I Am, your own divine, is here with you in every moment.

* * *

Now let's create an enlightenment toolbox, a collection of tools that can assist you along the way.

The first tool is *allowing*. Allowing means trusting in yourself, not doubting yourself. Allowing means understanding that this enlightenment is a natural process. It's going to happen anyway, no matter what. It's already designed into the soul, it's already there; simply allow it to happen. Take a deep breath and allow yourself.

The next tool is *passion*. Passion ignites energy; it's what energizes your life in any situation. Thinking and mental visualization has very little passion, so it doesn't call forth much energy.

The next tool, and a very useful one to remember, is *Point of Consciousness*, meaning the shift from one perspective to another without thinking about it. I call this Yo Soy el Punto, going to a different point.

One of the big distractions on the way to enlightenment is the human idea that you're not going to have any problems when you're enlightened. The truth is, as long as you're living here in this physical reality, there will still be problems, simply because there are other people.

There will still be the seduction drama, but instead of having it draw you in and consume you, you'll be able to say, "Oh, drama! I'm just going to be in that experience for a little while and then I'll choose to be out. I'll change my point of consciousness, Yo Soy el Punto, and simply step out of that. It's just an experience."

You're used to changing your Point of Consciousness by thinking. You don't like being unhealthy, so you think, "How am I going to get healthy?" There's no passion in that, just mental thought question, and it actually gets you more stuck.

Instead, you can say, "I'm in this Point of Consciousness of being unhealthy," and then take a deep breath and simply go over to the Point of Consciousness of being healthy.

In other words, if you have a health issue, simply take a deep breath and start acting like you're healthy. That's it. That is changing from one Point of Consciousness to another. You just start acting, which changes your perception, which changes the way energy is brought in, which then changes your reality. You don't think your way into this Point of Consciousness; you *become* it. That's why I say, "Yo Soy el Punto; I Am the Point of Consciousness that I choose."

In the past, you tried to think through it and got stuck. Now, just imagine it like hopping over to a different star. You're just there. You allow a change in perspective and it changes the way energy is brought in. *Just act it. Yo Soy el Punto. I Am the Point of Consciousness.*

If there is a problem in your life – relationship, abundance, or anything else – first of all, be aware of the energy in this problem. Instead of thinking, "Oh, what can I do about this problem?" just take a moment and be conscious of it.

Then, instead of trying to solve the problem in your mind, just remove the power from it. It has a power dynamic; just take the power out of that problem.

And now, come to this Point of Consciousness, the Yo Soy el Punto, and be where you want to be, without the problem. It's that simple. Don't think about the problem; come to that new place where it doesn't exist.

And then, *allow* the new reality to come in. And it will. It now has the energy. You've made a choice. You're aware at a very loving, compassionate level of what the problem was, and now just come into that new reality. It's that simple.

Let's say you're constantly getting a sore throat. Don't sit and think about the reason why or say, "I must be getting sore throats because I'm not letting my real voice out," because now you're just getting mental. Simply be aware of that sore throat, take a deep breath and release the power.

Then you do the new Point of Consciousness – Yo Soy el Punto – of health. You jump over to the consciousness of balanced health, take a deep breath and feel the passion – "Ah! Healthy living! Integrated body!" That passion now starts bringing the energies of health to you and starts rebalancing your biology. You take a deep breath and allow these energies to serve you.

You don't think about it, worry about it or stress about it. You just allow. It's that simple. This is how, my dear friend, to live as an enlightened being. *It is so simple.*

Maybe you have an abundance problem. Oh, you've given so

much power to abundance! Even if you're in lack of abundance, that's giving power to it, particularly to money. There's some stuck energy there, be aware of it.

You don't have to talk to it, just be aware. "Ah, that's what it feels like." Get out of your head and just feel into it, and then pull the power out of it. You can say, "Power is an illusion. This doesn't need to have power."

You take a deep breath and simply change the Point of Consciousness. Instead of being in the "lack of abundance" consciousness, you jump over to that other star, the one of abundance without effort – "Yo Soy el Punto, I am the Point of Abundance!"

Feel that passion for a moment, the passion of energy, of money serving you. Imagine what you can do. Feel the passion, because that passion is what calls forth the energy.

Energies at every level in the neutral field – Earth, Cosmic, Crystal and Core – are all activated by your passion for abundance. Just get out of your way and allow it to happen. Don't think about it or wonder if you did it right. *Allow it*, and then it happens.

Perhaps you doubt yourself. Perhaps you don't love or honor yourself. Like the other problems, that lack of self-worth is a type of entity. It is made up of your ghosts and demons, those aspects who taunt and ridicule you, and there is more power tied up in this than almost any other problem. You've given it a lot of power. You doubt yourself, loathe yourself and limit yourself in so many ways.

It doesn't really matter why you've done that – maybe just for the experience – but the fact is that you did.

Now be aware of this lack of self-worth and compassion for yourself. You give compassion to everybody else, but forget to give it to yourself. Feel into it. Not thinking about it, but feeling it. It has a resonance.

Now, take away the illusion of power that you've given it. Yes, you can release the power. It will try to tell you that you can't, that this is just a stupid game, but stand up for yourself.

Choose for yourself.

Be yourself. Take the power right out of this.

You created it; you can un-create it right now.

Take a deep breath.

Now go to this new Point of Consciousness – Yo Soy el Punto, the I Am, the compassion of the soul. "I Am that I Am. I exist. Therefore, nothing has power over me, including all these aspects. I Am that I Am. This is what I choose."

Feel yourself at this new Point of Consciousness where you have an awareness of yourself through the eyes of compassion, honor, acceptance and love.

Feel that passion – the passion of loving yourself – filling you and then overflowing back over yourself, falling in love with yourself again and again and again.

Feel the passion of being with your Self; you and your spirit.

This passion brings forth all of the energies – Core, Crystal, Cosmic and Earth – to create the reality, the experience of loving yourself again and again and again.

Finally, just accept that you can love yourself, that you can have health and abundance and relationships, that you can have joy, and allow it to become so.

Take a deep breath.

It is this simple.

IV

IT IS TIME

~ 16 ~

The Merlin Effect

Merlin was not one person. Merlin was a title taken on by numerous Masters over the ages. Most people are familiar with the Merlin of Camelot dating back to the 4th and 5th centuries, but the Merlin title was first used around 600 BCE. A Merlin has been present in Europe and the Mideast ever since then until the 17th century, most notably in the areas of Romania, France, England, Hungary and Austria. The Merlins of the time worked closely with the Mystery Schools. They were known for their ability to time-travel and shape-shift. When a Merlin of one era would meet a Merlin of another era in their time-travels, they would acknowledge each other with the greeting, "Oh-Be-Ahn." There have not been any embodied Merlins for the past 400 years.

The Merlin Effect is based on spiritual physics that anyone can experience. Merlin was able to travel forward and backward through time. Merlin's Future Self would come to visit his (or her) Past or Present Self, not in an attempt to alter anything, but rather to remind that all is well. It's a remarkable and simple concept that can dramatically affect the sense of grace and wellbeing in your life.

Time traveling into your past is a profound experience. It also requires a tremendous amount of compassion, which is an absolute honoring of what is. You will encounter yourself as a child, teenager or young adult, oftentimes at a point of trauma. And, because it's you, there's a tendency to either get caught up in the emotion and drama, or to try to fix the situation. But the Merlin Effect is not about altering the past. It is about making a compassionate visit into the past *as an observer*.

You don't even need to say a word to your Past Self. Just be in your radiance, your I Am Presence, and this simple act will be felt by your Past Self. It will feel like it was visited by an amazing loving angel at a time of great challenge or duress, and in fact it was. The amazing angel was you – from the future, from now. Your compassionate presence lets your Past Self know that everything is okay, that all is well. And suddenly your Present Self will realize that there was so much more to that previous traumatic experience than what your mind had remembered. The mind had filtered out the fullness and richness of the experience, focusing instead on the trauma, but there was so much more richness to the experience.

You can time travel to more than just traumatic events in your past. You can visit your Past Self when you were playing with friends, taking a walk by yourself in the forest or daydreaming at school. Each time you travel to your past, bringing your radiance and compassion, a new wisdom is birthed for both your Past Self and your Present Self.

What happens then is what Tobias said years ago: *The future is the past healed.* When you time travel to your past in compassion, it heals and releases the trauma points, thereby allowing you to see new potentials for the future because you're no longer bound by the limitations or grief of the past.

You can also experience the Merlin Effect from your Future Self to your Present Self. Your Future Self is probably already doing this with you; it's only a matter of becoming aware of it.

To do this, find a quiet space and spend about ten minutes in conscious breathing and relaxing. Then simply allow yourself to feel the presence of your Future Self. Just as you did when time traveling to your Past Self, your Future Self will be there with you in compassionate radiance. It (you) won't say any words because they would be meaningless. But you can feel the love, grace and wisdom of your Future Self in your present moment. The experience is nearly indescribable. Feeling the presence of the Master that you are in the future will remind you that you are already a Master today.

It is time that you go beyond *time*. As you break out of the limitations of the three-dimensional reality, you begin to realize that your past is not what you remembered it to be. You realize that the Master is not only in the future. The Master – you – is here now and was also in every moment in your past. You realize that embodied enlightenment is not something you are striving for because it is already here, albeit from something you call the future.

The timelessness of experiencing the Merlin Effect will help you to understand that it all works out, that *all is well*. You can do this experience with yourself any time you want, into your past or from your future. Just remember to always be in compassion. You're not trying to fix anything, because nothing is broken.

After experiencing the Merlin Effect in your life, you'll come to understand that enlightenment has already happened. Now, how do you choose to experience getting there or realizing it? It has already happened at a Point of Consciousness that you the human would call the future. So now, how do you choose to experience getting there?

Feel into this Merlin Effect experience, whether later today, next month or three months from now, but at some other point in the future. Feel deeply into it; not the details of how you got there, but the realization; not a specific event, but the true feeling.

It has already happened. It is already here. *What does it feel like?*

Feel the passion of the soul that has brought enlightenment into this human realm.

Feel into this life-changing experience – the essence, the beauty, the grace, the unfolding.

This is not a prophecy or a prediction. It's not destiny or the result of astrological events. It is simply the passion of the soul as it integrates deeply with the human.

It is nothing that has been inflicted or imposed upon you. It is because of your choice for enlightenment and your *allowing* it to become so.

Don't worry about how you got to enlightenment or try to discern the events leading up to it. Simply feel into the realization, the awareness of the experience.

Please… put this book down for about five minutes and feel into the passion of your soul. It already IS enlightened; feel it now as it comes to you.

~ 17 ~

Walk Like a Master

Energy responds to the act of consciousness. This means that energy literally aligns itself to your consciousness. Most people aren't conscious of their consciousness. They might be aware of their thoughts, but really being aware of your consciousness is more of a feeling. And that's what energy responds to, because real feeling, what I call sensory intelligence – the physical human senses *and* the senses of the I Am – has passion to it. Whether it is sadness and depression or happiness and joy, whether it's abundance or lack, there is a passion to it, a radiance. And that radiance is what calls in the energies – the quantity of energy, the type of energy, and the particular balance of negative and positive particles – that manifest reality.

It is your passion and radiance that create reality, not the mind or thought. That's why I've never been a fan of affirmations; they're very mental. If you try to change your reality through affirmations, you'll end up getting frustrated, thinking you're not very good at creation. No, it's because affirmations are mental and don't have much passion to them.

I'm also not a fan of what's called the Law of Attraction. The principle is good, but the execution tends to be much more mental than passionate. As a matter of fact, there's a lot of fear around the Law of Attraction – "Oh my god! I'm going to attract the wrong thing into my life. I better not do anything. I better hide! I might think the wrong thought." Actually, thoughts are not very potent because there's not much energy in them. But the fear of doing it wrong – ah, now that has passion to it! It is the attraction or magnetism of passion that actually creates reality, regardless of what the passion is about or the thoughts behind it.

Energy responds to the act, the expression of consciousness. Even when you're not so conscious of your consciousness, energy is still responding. Even if your consciousness is low and hiding, energy is responding accordingly.

What to do? Well, you can talk about it, you can think about it, or you can act upon it. How do you act upon it? Well, let's start with something very, very basic: walking. It gets you out of your mind a little bit and into your body. It gets some feeling going. Walking is a great way to begin acting like a Master, even if you're just acting, even if you think it's totally fake. The fact that you're doing it and allowing it changes the energy dynamics.

So, stand up now and start walking as if you are already a Master. It may feel a little awkward and uncomfortable at first. It may feel like, "Oh, this really isn't me." Yes, actually, it is, if you choose it to be. Do you really want to be a Master? Then start walking like one.

You see, the energy will respond even if you're just faking it, because, well, it's *all* fake. It's all an illusion. It's all an act. Pretty soon you'll begin to see that everything up to now has been an act – a beautiful, well-played, well-orchestrated act supported by energy and other people – but still just an act.

The real reason you hold back or feel anxious and concerned about it is because it works. "Oh my gosh, I really *can* change my reality! It really is this easy. Maybe I shouldn't do anything just yet, because I might get it wrong." But remember, you're at a place of consciousness where you can't do the wrong thing. You really can't. It is just part of living. It's just an experience.

Put this book down now and take a little walk around the room. Give yourself a real experience of walking like a Master.

* * *

Now, you'll notice, even if you're just acting, a few things show up right away. You walk a little straighter, a little taller, with a little more consciousness than your usual shuffling steps. If you do this around others you'll also notice there is more eye contact with them. You'll notice that things that might have been a little frightening or intimidating suddenly seem much easier. It's a little disconcerting perhaps, but fun at the same time. There's something different in the way the energy comes in when you walk like a Master. Even if you're just faking it, the energy flows different.

This is where it becomes real, if you choose. Actually go out and walk around like a Master for a while. Allow yourself to feel it, to actually do it. Observe how it feels, how people respond to you, how life feels all around you. Notice the difference when you walk like a Master.

You might like to do it first in nature. There it's easy to openly walk like a Master, because you know the trees will not steal your energy and the ground will not suck you in. It's a harmonious environment. When you open your awareness in some place like a shopping mall or a train station, it can be a little painful at first, because there's a concern that other people's psychic energy might start attacking you. It won't. It might try, it might play around a little bit, but ultimately, it won't. In fact, you'll discover that other people's energy, their consciousness, will actually honor you. They'll admire you.

When you walk like a Master, the senses open up. You see more, hear more and feel more. Everything opens up, if that's what you want.

When you really let yourself get into the act and walk like a Master, your breathing changes. It gets a little deeper, a little more intentional. When you act and walk like a Master, you literally take in more oxygen. Your body actually absorbs more life force energy than if you're just walking and acting like a limited human. You're literally opening up and allowing for more energy to come into the physical body.

As you do that, more and more Cosmic energy and then Crystal energy will come in. And, ultimately, your Core energy will come in. You'll find that you don't need to derive as much energy from things like food or sunlight, but if you do partake of them, your body knows how to stay in balance.

When you walk like a Master, you start breathing like a Master. Right now, your breathing is shallow, the body taking in just what it needs to get by. When you walk like a Master, your body and even the air around you respond accordingly. You bring more in and your body literally absorbs more of the energies that come in with the air. You won't be so tired, the additional oxygen clears up the brain and thoughts, and then it's even easier to walk like a Master.

Play around with this. Walk like a Master wherever you go. Notice the difference in your breathing, in how you feel. Eat like a Master. Oh, Masters, they can eat a lot! Experience the difference in the awareness of everything – the tastes, the noises around you, what you're doing, how you're feeling – everything.

Walk like a Master in your act of consciousness.

~ 18 ~

What Goes On Earth

The eyes of creation, in both the physical and nonphysical dimensions, are watching from all around the cosmos. Your angelic families are watching what happens on Earth right now. You, as a leader of your angelic family, came to this place of Earth, infused it with life force energies and dived in. Now your angelic family is watching to see how you fared, to see if you can truly remember your angelic origins, and to see if you come to have an intimate and loving relationship with the grandness of your I Am heritage.

From all around creation, souled beings are watching to see how humanity will deal with the issues of energy and freedom.

Humans are finally learning about energy. It looks like a crisis – a literal energy crisis with your fuel supplies – but it's really about learning how to work with energies, how to call them forth and how to have them serve you.

Humans are also working on the issue of freedom. In a limited state of consciousness, there is very little freedom. In a mental hypnotic state, there is very little freedom. But now, something is changing. Humans all over the world are talking about freedom, even rioting for freedom. There are many, such as yourself, who are awakening and, in doing so, beginning to realize the importance of sovereignty and freedom in their lives. They want freedom, not just from governments and corporations, but true freedom within themselves. Awakening humans like you are seeking freedom from limited beliefs, old hypnotic overlays, mental programming and freedom from the past.

Indeed, the eyes of the universe are watching what goes on Earth.

You're going to see a new cycle of increased activity from other beings, entities from distant places and dimensions. It doesn't mean they're just going to descend here in their spaceships. They project themselves here through other means than metal spacecraft, but there will be increased alien activity because they're wondering, "What is going on with the humans? What are they choosing?"

These other entities are intrigued by this thing you call love. Love was first experienced here on this planet and they're curious about it. They wonder if it's contained in the physical body or in the mind, but when they probe and investigate, they can't find it. "What is it? Where does it come from? How did humans create it and how do they experience it?"

Even Spirit did not know love until you, as humans, experienced it. Love is the gift from humanity to all Creation.

These beings from other places are wondering what it's like to dive so deep into the density of physical reality that you forget who you are. They wonder how you can emerge out of this Earth density all on your own without any outside assistance, so they're watching, paying close attention to what you're going through.

I tell you this so that you understand the importance of what you're doing. You're doing it for yourself of course, but there are huge implications for the rest of Creation. You're going through this experience for yourself, but what you do, what you experience, and how you come to know yourself has vast implications.

You are no longer an energy holder; you're a bringer of the New Energy. You're not here to maintain energy balances on Earth anymore. There are others who have stepped up to that role, who are doing it now. You are a bringer of the New Energy, a bringer of the new consciousness.

Sometimes, it's a very lonely journey. Sometimes, the human mind wants to go into action and say, "I have to *do something* to save the planet." But you already are. Through what you're doing, through this passion for awakening within the experience of being human, you are bringing in new potentials for this planet.

It's amazing – absolutely quantum amazing – what you're doing, and I know there are times when you don't really realize it or understand. There are times when you think you're failing, especially when the outside world doesn't reflect what's really going on inside. But you are making tremendous strides.

Hear these words. *You are exactly where you should be, not a moment too soon or a moment too late. All is well.*

~ 19 ~

The Last Battle

I will be with you every step of the way into your enlightenment. Make no mistake that it is you doing this for yourself, but I will be with you every step of the way.

They are joyful steps for me, and I know they are sometimes challenging and difficult steps for you. But I will be with you.

My message at the end of this living book is short and simple: the last battle has been fought. The war is finally over. The battles have been within yourself; the war has been about duality, self-perception, self-acceptance and self-love. But now the conflicts are over and done with.

As with the end of any battle or war, now the rejuvenation comes. Within the reality landscape there are things to rebuild, energies to clear out, tears to be shed, memories to be felt. But as with any war, when it is finally done, the fields renew and rejuvenate themselves. The trees come back to life. The skies clear so that the sun and endless blue can be seen again. The smoke fades away.

And such it has been with your experience as a human on this planet, an experience that has led you deep into the act of consciousness, into beingness, into forgetting who you truly are; an experience that, as you emerged, caused these wars within. But now they are a thing of the past.

These battles have given you amazing insights and significant understandings about the *I Am that I Am*. They have brought tremendous wisdom to your soul. And now they are over.

Now you enter into your new life – a life as a being of peace, a being who understands how to use energy, who understands compassion for self and compassion for all others.

You enter into a life that is filled with abundance, self-love, health and clarity.

You enter into a life that is by your own choosing, not by the dictates of any other beings – human or otherwise.

You enter into a life that is filled with grace, the life of a Master who allows energies to serve them. This is the definition of grace – allowing energies to serve you, finally.

Humanity is in the New Energy era. We talked about Core energies, those closest to your soul, your consciousness. We talked about the Crystalline energies, those high birthing energies of great beauty and majesty. We talked about the Cosmic energies that come from all places and realms in physical creation. And we talked about Earth energies, the ones you have been playing in for so very long.

Now there is one more to behold and that is the New Energy.

This New Energy does not come from the reservoir or pool of the old energies. It is truly new. It combines your consciousness and energy into a single element. Consciousness and energy have always been separate. But now, in this new era, they can be brought together into something magnificent and new.

You created energy from the desire of your consciousness and then separated it from yourself. But now you bring it together, integrated and melded into one essence. You bring it into your everyday life, into your heart. You bring it to this planet so that others may also bring in their own when the time is right for them. You bring it, as you bring any energy into your life, simply with the breath and the act of consciousness.

The New Energy is all yours, altogether, and, like consciousness itself, it can never be corrupted. It can never be taken by another. It can never be extinguished. It is the crystal flame that is always, always burning, always yours.

Behold what you have brought into your life. Yes, the road has been difficult, but also filled with incredible experience and depth that few other angels will ever have. Behold all that you have brought into this new life of yours – wisdom, love, compassion and indeed New

Energy – energy and consciousness together, not from Spirit, not even from the great Field of energy, but something you created for yourself.

Go forth, whether it is an act or not, with love for yourself in your heart.

Go forth as a teacher, a poet, an artist, an engineer, or anything you choose to be. Go forth and, like the Ascended Masters who are coming back to Earth now, allow yourself to enjoy life. Allow yourself many long years on this planet, years filled with abundance, grace and honor.

Go forth breathing in the energies, breathing in this New Energy that you have created.

Take this moment, at these final pages, to behold all that you have done, all that you have given and now, all that you receive.

I Am Adamus Saint-Germain, in loving service to you.

Other Books by Geoffrey Hoppe
with Adamus Saint-Germain and Tobias

Memoirs of a Master – *Adamus Saint-Germain*
Stories of Spiritual Realization – A collection of stories based on real-life encounters between Adamus Saint-Germain and his students. These simple stories can be experienced on many different levels ranging from profound wisdom to very human, insightful and humorous realizations.

Live Your Divinity – *Adamus Saint-Germain*
A new dimension in spiritual teaching, this intriguing and provocative book will challenge your perceptions of reality, remind you of forgotten truths, and prod you toward the realization and manifestation of your divine nature here on Earth.

Masters in the New Energy – *Adamus Saint-Germain*
This profound and delightful book is filled with insightful and practical information about living as true Masters in the New Energy. Adamus' simple and profound messages provide the guideposts for those who choose to go beyond limited thoughts and beliefs into a new understanding of reality.

Journey of the Angels – *Tobias*
Learn how and why we became separated from Spirit, what transpires in the angelic realms, and discover a new and refreshing picture of why Earth was created and why we chose to come here. This profound material will reawaken memories that have been buried since the beginning and help you remember the answers to the most basic questions about life. *Journey of the Angels* speaks to the deepest parts

of you and will awaken you to the divine purpose that brought you into this lifetime.

Creator Series – *Tobias*

"*You never go Home. Instead, Home comes to you.*" With these words Tobias laid out an entirely new understanding of how we came to Earth and why this is such an important crossroads on our spiritual journey. The Creator Series is full of practical tools for thriving as an awakening being on Earth.

Other Courses
with Adamus Saint-Germain

DreamWalker™ Death Transitions
This three-day school, offered by certified teachers, teaches how to guide friends, family and clients through the death process into the non-physical realms, providing comfort and love to make their transition more peaceful. This School offers certification as a DreamWalker Death Guide.

DreamWalker™ Birth Transitions
This three-day school is offered by certified teachers as well as through a Personal Study Course. Saint-Germain defines the birth process from conception to post-birth with a focus on the spiritual selection aspects. This School offers certification as a DreamWalker "Adoula" Guide.

DreamWalker™ Ascension Transitions
Adamus Saint-Germain's three day Ascension School provides unique and personal insights into the nature of Ascension and the implications of the last lifetime on Earth. This course is offered by certified DreamWalker Ascension teachers.

DreamWalker™ Life
Adamus Saint-Germain's three day DreamWalker Life School provides insights on how to truly live in and love life. Through Quantum Allowing and the grace of the crystal flame of transfiguration, attendees learn what it means to be a Master on Earth. This course is offered by certified DreamWalker DreamWalker Life teachers.

New Energy Synchrotize™
Adamus Saint-Germain says Synchrotize goes "beyond hypnosis"

for those who want to consciously create their reality. Synchrotize is offered as a Personal Study Course. The study process takes four consecutive days to complete.

Standard Technology

Adamus Saint-Germain and Tobias join together to present Standard Technology, a New Energy program for activating your body's natural rejuvenation system. Standard Technology is offered as a Personal Study Course.

Additional Courses and Material
available through the Crimson Circle

Tobias' Sexual Energies School
This three-day school focuses on what Tobias calls the "sexual energy virus." It helps the student understand how people energetically feed off of each other, and how to release the chain of the virus. This is one of the most basic and important courses offered by the Crimson Circle. It is taught by certified teachers worldwide.

Tobias' Aspectology School
In this three-day workshop, Tobias focuses on the Aspects or parts of self that negatively affect and sometimes control our lives due to trauma, whether in this or a past life. Learn tools to help you integrate these energies and bring true freedom to your life. This core material is taught by certified Crimson Circle teachers worldwide.

Tobias' Journey of the Angels School
In this profound school, given three weeks before his departure, Tobias weaves together the core of all his teachings over the previous 10 years. Offering a completely different perspective on everything you learned in church and school, this school will change your concept of what being human really is.

Single and Multi-Session Audio Products Tobias, Kuthumi and Adamus cover a broad range of topics in dozens of recorded presentation. Varying in length from an hour or less to 15 or more hours of channeling, these life-changing sessions are also available with translations in nearly 20 languages.

Monthly Shouds Text transcripts or audio recordings of all channeled monthly messages since August 1999 are available *free of* *charge* on the Crimson Circle web site (www.crimsoncircle.com). The Shouds are channeled in annual series (The Creator Series, The New Earth Series, The Divine Human Series, etc.) and also include many Question and Answer sessions. The Shouds are an excellent record of Shaumbra's journey since the beginning of the Crimson Circle.

Workshops Geoffrey and Linda Hoppe present workshops around the world featuring live channelings with Adamus Saint-Germain, Kuthumi and Merlin. Check the Crimson Circle web site for dates and details.

www.crimsoncircle.com

About Adamus Saint-Germain

Saint-Germain (also sometimes referred to as Master Rakoczi) is a spiritual Master of the Ancient Wisdom credited with mystical powers and longevity. He is also identified with the real life person known as the Count of St. Germain (1710–1784) who lived throughout Europe in the 18th century and was active in many of the Mystery Schools of the time. He adopted his name as a French version of the Latin "Sanctus Germanus," meaning "Holy Brother." Saint-Germain teaches that the highest alchemy is the transformation of one's human consciousness into the divinity of the Higher Self.

Over the years, much has been written and many stories told of this intriguing, somewhat enigmatic figure in history. He is a remarkable being who has manifested in many lifetimes and identities on Earth. In his lifetime as St. Germain, he was born in an area now known as Spain to a Jewish Portuguese father and a mother of royal Spanish lineage. He traveled throughout Europe counseling kings and other royalty, and was known as a great alchemist – a great mover of energy.

In 2005 Saint-Germain came to the Crimson Circle organization as a guest of Tobias, another Ascended Master, channeled by Geoffrey Hoppe. After Tobias' reincarnation to the physical realms in July 2009, Saint-Germain took over his teaching and guidance role with the Crimson Circle. In his work with the Crimson Circle, he refers to himself as Adamus Saint-Germain in order to differentiate his contemporary teachings related to embodied ascension from his previous work and previous channelers. Adamus is a unique facet of Saint-Germain's oversoul. His style is provocative, entertaining and deeply insightful. His passion is to assist those who have clearly chosen embodied enlightenment in this lifetime, yet are faced with the myriad distractions and doubts that stem from today's intense mental focus and programming coupled with the density of mass consciousness.

About Geoffrey Hoppe

Geoffrey A. Hoppe was born and raised in the Midwest United States in a large Catholic family. His interest in spirituality and metaphysics started at the age of 19 when he hypnotized a friend. While in a trance state the friend began to recount a series of previous lifetimes. Geoffrey immersed himself into the study of metaphysics and religion for the next several years.

His spiritual journey was all but forgotten for nearly 20 years with the demands of his business career. Geoffrey worked for several advertising agencies and manufacturing companies in the Midwest and Texas in senior marketing positions. At age 28 he started a marketing consulting company in Dallas, Texas, operating it for 12 years with industrial and high tech clients throughout the United States. He co-founded an aviation telecommunications company where he served as Vice President of Sales and Marketing until 2001. Geoff holds two U.S. patents and one international patent for multidimensional telecommunications technologies, and numerous trademarks and copyrights.

Tobias first presented himself to Geoffrey in 1997 on an airplane flight and they "talked" for nearly a year before Geoffrey channeled Tobias for another person. Tobias provided deep insights into their past lives and current challenges and, after his return to the physical realms in 2009, Geoffrey now channels Adamus Saint-Germain.

Geoffrey founded the Crimson Circle in 1999, and it quickly developed an international audience. He currently delivers messages from several angelic beings, including Adamus Saint-Germain, Kuthumi lal Singh and Merlin. Geoffrey has been married to Linda Benyo, his high school sweetheart, since 1977. They have been partners in life and business ever since. When they are not traveling and teaching around the world, they live in the Rocky Mountains outside of Golden, Colorado, USA.

About Linda Benyo Hoppe

Even as a young child, Linda loved to draw angels. In grade school she won a city-wide art contest for one of her angel drawings, and went on to earn a degree in Art Education, graduating Summa Cum Laude from the University of Wisconsin.

Linda taught Art Education in Wisconsin and Texas. During her time in Texas she wrote a ground-breaking curriculum for the state's first high school honors Art Education program. After seven years of teaching, Linda's talents were noticed by a Fortune 500 retail company with over 1000 stores across the US. In her role as Fashion Merchandise Manager she traveled around the world with the company's buyers to select clothing designs and styles for the coming seasons. Places like India, Nepal and Indonesia made a lasting impression on her.

Linda took over management of her husband Geoffrey's marketing consulting company at a time when he was occupied with a start-up technology company. With business-to-business clients across the southwest US, she ran the business until the Crimson Circle became a full-time venture for both of them in 2003.

Linda and Geoffrey work closely together when Adamus and other angelic beings to deliver their messages. As the channeler, Geoffrey expands his consciousness into the non-physical realms and receives "thought packets," which he then translates into words for others to hear. Linda, sitting beside him, also helps bring in the message and holds an important energetic balance between the angelic beings, Geoffrey, and the audience. They find that this team approach keeps the message clear and grounded even as they venture into expanded forms of consciousness.

Linda has received acclaim from listeners and viewers around the world for her group breathing experiences. She leads the breathing for all Crimson Circle gatherings, helping to balance the energies and create a safe space for personal transformation. She considers this to be one of her greatest joys.

About The Crimson Circle

The Crimson Circle Energy Company, Inc., based in Golden, Colorado USA, is a global affiliation of New Energy teachers. The teachers are experienced metaphysicians, healers and spiritual counselors coming from all walks of life, a wide variety of spiritual backgrounds, and from over 130 countries around the world.

The Crimson Circle offers holistic and spiritual lifestyle messages, products and services. One of the primary purposes is to support the worldwide group of affiliate teachers, called "Shaumbra," unified in their process of spiritual awakening, teaching and living. The Crimson Circle has an open belief system that honors all people and their diverse beliefs, and does not subscribe to limitations involving the human condition.

The Crimson Circle began in 1999 based on the inspired messages of Tobias. Tobias is best known for his lifetime over 2,500 years ago as portrayed in the apocryphal Book of Tobit. He brought his messages, wisdom and humor delivered through Geoffrey Hoppe for ten years, offering assistance to those who are going through the process of spiritual transformation and those who choose to be New Energy teachers. Since Tobias returned to Earth in July 2009, Geoffrey now delivers messages from ascended Masters Adamus Saint-Germain and Kuthumi lal Singh.

The Crimson Circle is known as the "Classroom of the New Spiritual Energy." The group works with the dynamics of psycho-spiritual empowerment and enlightenment, integrating their personal divinity and humanity, and embracing their spirit within. The Crimson Circle is about discovering that "You Are God Also" and experiencing life with a new sense of purpose, passion and joy.

There are now hundreds of local Shaumbra groups, over 300,000 visitors per month to the Crimson Circle web site and over 25 international language websites. Visit the Crimson Circle web site at www.crimsoncircle.com for more information.

Glossary

Adamus Saint–Germain – A master, an angel, a professor and a teacher from the Crimson Council who is delivering inspiring messages for New Energy consciousness.

Anayatron – The communication network that all energy particles use to communicate with all other energy particles, particularly within the Body of Consciousness.

Angel – A souled being, birthed from the original Oneness, created by the love of Spirit.

Ascended Master – A souled being who has completed their journey of lifetimes on Earth, accepted their own sovereignty and fully integrated every part and expression of their soul in complete love and acceptance.

Ascension – The state of being wholly and completely in acceptance and love for oneself without reservation, having let go of all limitations of the human existence and being fully integrated with every part of Self.

Aspects (Aspectology™) – Different roles or identities we as Creator Beings have used to answer the question: Who Am I? We create aspects of ourselves to meet situations in this lifetime (e.g. the child, the parent, the business owner, the healer, etc). We also have many other aspects from past lives, from dreams and from the multidimensional realms. When aspects become "stuck" they can cause chaos and confusion as they move in and out of consciousness. However, through conscious choice, we can welcome these aspects back home within ourselves and become fully integrated.

Atlantis – The second era of Earth experience, coming after the Lemurian era. Atlanteans were very communal by nature and did extensive work to standardize the human mind and body.

Cauldre – The name Tobias and Adamus Saint-Germain call Geoffrey Hoppe. This is not his "spirit name," rather a nickname used. Pronounced Ka–ool'–dra.

Channeling – When a nonphysical entity or angel communicates through a human. The human translates the entity's "thought packets" into words for others to hear or read.

Compassion – Total acceptance and allowing of what is; including unconditional love for self, and absolute honor for the path and choices of others.

Crimson Circle – The group of humans involved in this spiritual journey, preparing to become teachers to others on the journey.

Crimson Council – A celestial teaching order, including Tobias, Adamus Saint–Germain, and other angels, assisting us on our journey.

Enlightenment – The realization of being wholly and completely in acceptance and love for yourself without reservation, having let go of all limitations of the human existence and fully integrated with every part of Self.

Ica – According to Adamus, an *ica* has similar qualities to a photon and is the smallest particle that can be affected by consciousness in 3D reality. Ignited by consciousness and passion, light and ica particles bring reality into being.

Makyo – Spiritual verbiage and platitudes that distract from the true experience of Self. Adamus also describes this as 'spiritual bullshit.'

New Energy – The new consciousness and vibration of Earth that allows the integration of our divine nature into our human nature. Also, the transition from the physics of "duality" or "2" into the "quad physics" or energy of "4."

Shaumbra – The name Tobias uses for the group of humans going through the awakening process. Tobias tells us the term originated during the times of Yeshua ben Joseph (Jesus), when people, many of them Essenes, would gather for spiritual meetings. Loosely translated in old Hebrew, the first portion of the word Shaumbra is pronounced "shau–home." "Shau–home" means home or family. The second portion of the term is "ba–rah," which means journey and mission. When these terms are put together, it is "shau–home–ba–rah" which means family that is on a journey and experience together. Tobias says that in the biblical times, a "shaumbra" was also a scarf or shawl that was worn by either male or female. It was a distinctive crimson color that let the others know it was time to meet. Pronounced "Shom–bra."

Spirit – Also called God, Source or the Eternal One, the divine spark that is within each souled being.

"All is well in all of Creation"

- Adamus Saint-Germain

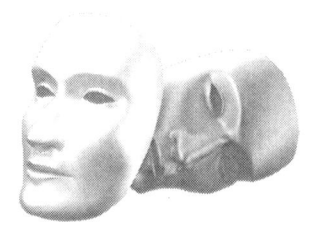

Notes

Notes

Notes

Notes

Notes

Notes

Notes

Notes